OLD TRAILS AND FRONTIERS

Lincolnshire
COUNTY COUNCIL

discover libraries
This book should be returned on or before the last date shown below.

LA1

To renew or order library books please telephone 01522 782010
or visit www.lincolnshire.gov.uk
You will require a Personal Identification Number
Ask any member of staff for this.

EC. 199 (LIBS): RS/L5/19

OLD TRAILS AND FRONTIERS

Driving the American Southwest

William Croft

Book Guild Publishing

Sussex, England

First published in Great Britain in 2012 by
The Book Guild Ltd
Pavilion View
19 New Road
Brighton, BN1 1UF

Copyright © William Croft 2012

The right of William Croft to be identified as the author of
this work has been asserted by him in accordance with the
Copyright, Designs and Patents Act 1988.

Typesetting in Garamond by
MRM Graphics Ltd, Winslow, Bucks

Printed in Spain under the supervision of
MRM Graphics Ltd, Winslow Bucks

A catalogue record for this book is available from
The British Library.

ISBN 978 1 84624 655 5

Contents

List of Maps

The maps are not drawn to an accurate scale. They are simple and easy reference points for the drives described in the chapters. For back-up have a good atlas in the car. In recent years I have used *Mapquest, Roadmaster 2005, Standard Road Atlas, United States-Canada-Mexico* which is excellent for use with this book.

Abbreviations in the text and on the maps

BLM	Bureau of Land Management
NCA	National Conservation Area
NHP	National Historic Park
NHS	National Historic Site
NM	National Monument
NP	National Park
NPS	National Park Service
NS	National Seashore
SHP	State Historic Park
SHM	State Historic Monument
SP	State Park

Acknowledgements

The author and publishers have made every effort to obtain permission to reproduce any images in this book that are not the property of the author. The publisher will be pleased to correct omissions in any subsequent printings.

Introduction

Most British people who visit the American Southwest go no further than the gateway cities they use to get there. Los Angeles has Hollywood and Disneyland; San Francisco has its Golden Gate Bridge, Alcatraz and Fisherman's Wharf; and Las Vegas its fabulous theme parks, shows and casinos. But travellers with a real wanderlust and who love driving the open road go much further afield than this, and for good reason. The Southwest is truly a driver's paradise!

An incredible richness of wilderness scenery dominates the Southwest. Monument Valley is its most iconic landscape; Grand Canyon, Canyonlands and Zion are imperious, majestic and mysterious; Arches, Bryce Canyon and Yosemite exude a natural architecture of artistry and grace. Saguaro, ocotillo and other prickly and colourful cacti and the lovely yellow and blue paloverde trees characterise the exotic and bizarre landscape of the Sonora Desert. To the northwest there are endless forests of Douglas fir and Ponderosa pine, and majestic groves of coastal redwoods and mighty sequoias. The blue Pacific and Coast Ranges of California mingle land, sea and sky into lovely vistas at almost every turn of the road. Such places remain homes to the golden eagle, raven, black bear, mountain lion, desert bighorn, coyote, mule deer, lizard and rattlesnake. Generally, wherever you are and whatever the season, blue skies and white clouds usually stand over the earth, the grandeur enhanced at dawn and sunset and in stormy weather when changing light and shadow weave their own magic on the land.

There is much more. The landscapes of the Southwest reflect a dramatic and dynamic human history profoundly different from Britain and Europe. They add a fascinating dimension to all of the drives. The wilderness still bears the indelible marks of prehistoric people like the Anasazi and the Hohokam; contemporary Indians such as the Navajo and the Hopi whose roots lie in the Stone Age; New World Spanish conquistadors, soldiers, missionaries and settlers; Mexican farmers and ranchers; persecuted Mormons fleeing west to build their new earthly Zion; American explorers, loggers, miners, homesteaders, cattlemen, railroaders, outlaws and gunfighters; and immigrant populations from places such as China and Eastern Europe. The names that ring out in the history of the Southwest are those of people like Coronado, Fathers Serra and Kino, Kit Carson, Brigham Young, John Muir, John Wesley Powell, Cochise and Geronimo, and Wyatt Earp and John Wayne.

The wilderness itself was a powerful dynamic shaping the nature and the course of the history of the Southwest. Seemingly infinite natural resources here made it yet another land of opportunity in America. Putting these resources to human use required individual action and corporate enterprise, physical strength and stamina, practical and mental ingenuity, privation and fortitude in the face of danger and adversity, great vision and planning, and an unwavering and boundless optimism about the future. Challenging the wilderness helped forge the American character and the American way of doing things.

American responses to the challenges of the wilderness are well known. Settlers and miners trekked overland across desert and mountain to California in search of fertile land and gold and a better life out west. The Central Pacific Railroad Company built its tracks, tunnels and snow-sheds over the high Sierra Nevada and across the desolate Great Basin. The mighty Hoover Dam was built to tame the wild Colorado River and to provide water and power for millions of Americans. But earlier peoples also overcame the wilderness in striking ways. All over the Colorado Plateau the prehistoric Anasazi Indians built multistorey stone complexes on mesa tops and in huge caves in the sides of high cliffs. Their pueblos (small towns) combined living areas with defined spaces for religion, work and play. Their contemporaries, the Hohokam, hand-dug hundreds of miles of canals and irrigated vast swathes of the Sonoran Desert in southern Arizona. To save the souls of the native Indians and to secure the northwestern frontier of their New World empire in North America, the Spanish built 21 missions along a track they called El Camino Real ('The Royal Road'), a dirt road some 600 miles long stretching through the coastal wilderness of California from San Diego to San Francisco. Each mission had its church, farm, gardens and orchards stocked with seeds, plants and animals from the Old World. The Mormons not only achieved the greatest single group migration in American history, but created their earthly paradise by irrigating a vast desert on the eastern side of the Great Salt Lake and building well-planned farms and model towns under the leadership of Brigham Young, one of the great colonisers of the Southwest.

Many of these outstanding natural and human landscapes are handsomely showcased in the parks and monuments of the exemplary National Park Service. They are the crown jewels in the wonderful wilderness lands of the Southwest. A century ago James Bryce, a British diplomat in America, said that national parks were the best idea America ever had and its greatest gift to the world. The NPS works to protect and conserve these landscapes for posterity and to educate people to understand their intrinsic value and place in America's natural and cultural heritage – a task brilliantly done so far. The pleasures of any drive in the Southwest are greatly enhanced by visits to these wonderful places. See as many as you can!

Every time you go to a park or monument, make sure to call at its Visitor Centre. Each has a first-rate audio-visual interpretation of its unique site, an excellent selection of books and other resources on sale, and well-signed interpretive walking trails of different lengths and degrees of difficulty. The ranger-led activities are wonderful learning experiences for adults as well as children. Their summer evening talks under starry skies and in the rosy glow of campfires are atmospheric and memorable. Note that most NPS parks and monuments have only basic facilities like drinking water and toilets. Only the biggest ones like Grand Canyon and Yosemite have accommodation, food stores and fuel.

The Southwest has an extensive network of well-paved highways and uncongested roads. Petrol, food and motels are relatively cheap. The fact that the locals speak a sort of English makes for engaging, puzzling and humorous conversations which hopefully maintain and enrich the Anglo-American alliance! In America you put gas in the car, drive on the pavement and walk on the sidewalk – if you can find one.

The American Southwest is an area at least four times bigger than the British Isles. The drives in this book follow roads that once were the great tracks and trails of past frontiers in the most scenic part of America. Most landscapes have changed little since these earlier times. Venturing there gives a great sense of adventure and discovery, and the open road and the far horizon offer a wonderful feeling of independence and freedom. If you love to drive in foreign places and this book excites you to explore the American Southwest, then I shall be thrilled. On the other hand, if you are an armchair traveller and enjoy reading this book, then that will please me too.

Map 1: Overview of the Southwest

1

Coast, Volcano and Wine

Northern California

A great drive of wonderful contrasts. The first 200 miles are dominated by increasingly rugged coastal scenery as you drive along the western flanks of the grassy and oak-studded Coast Ranges. Point Reyes NS, the state parks and 'The Lost Coast' protect much of the shoreline which has remained largely unchanged since Francis Drake's circumnavigation of the world in 1579.

Just north of Rockport, California 1 leaves the coast and climbs into the mountains to join US 101 at Leggatt. Northwards lie the 'Avenue of the Giants' and the Humboldt Redwoods SP. The coastal redwoods, the tallest trees in the world, stand here in large protected groves, instantly capturing all your senses.

East from Eureka, along California 299, magnificent forests of Douglas fir, Ponderosa pine and Sugar pine cover the Coast Ranges and the Klamath Mountains. Lassen Volcanic NP in the Cascade Range is spectacular. It has glaciated valleys, lakes and waterfalls, volcanoes, cinder cones, lava flows, boiling springs and mud-pots. During the short summer the main road through the park is open, climbing over 8,000 feet to give distant views of both the Cascades and the Sierra Nevada.

The final part of the drive ends in the county of Sonoma, part of the warm, balmy, luscious green pinstripe landscapes of northern California's wine country. The town of Sonoma retains some of the Hispanic atmosphere it had before California became the thirty-first state of America.

Suggested start/finish:	San Francisco
Length of journey:	About 750 miles; 6 or 7 days
Best time of year:	All year round for the coast and the wine country, but summer is the best time for Lassen Volcanic NP.
Weather:	Coast: mild winters with wind and rain; warm summers with fog belts along the coast.
	Inland to the north: in winter much rain on the

western slopes of the Coast Ranges and deep snows on the Cascades.

Wine country: a temperate Mediterranean climate with mild winters and some rain, and warm, dry summers with a strong possibility of fog.

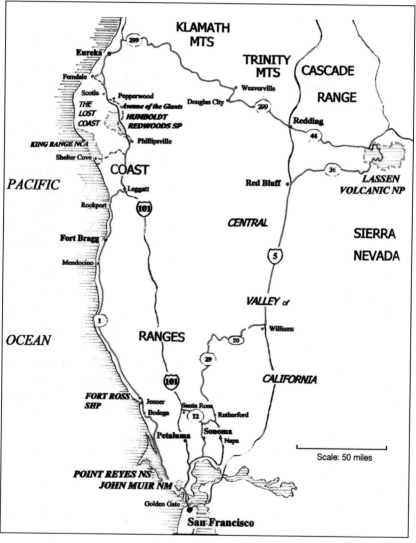

Map 2: Northern California

Drive highlights

San Francisco to Rockport (c. 195 miles)

Aptly named the 'Shoreline Highway', California 1 is a two-lane road that hugs the northern coastline and rightly compels an unhurried pace. For 200 miles the ocean is rarely out of view and the sea joins land and sky to make dramatic and inspiring landscapes, their natural beauty and solitude captured especially in the parks and monuments along the way. Whales and seals frequent the coastal waters and seabirds and red-tailed hawks fill the sky.

English, Spanish and Russian sea captains, missionaries, traders and colonisers were the earliest white visitors to this coastline, but it was the great California Gold Rush of 1849 that sparked its development. Logging, cattle ranching and fishing became important activities. Victorian mansions and houses and Western-style street fronts still give character and charm to the many new settlements that were established. Their authentic 'Americana' locations have attracted many Hollywood film productions. Alfred Hitchcock, for example, made *The Birds* at Bodega and James Dean starred in *East of Eden*, filmed in Mendocino. Many places are small and picturesque, sited in bays, near scenic estuaries or on cliff tops. Most have shops, boutiques, flea markets, restaurants specialising in seafood and foreign cuisines, and rooms to rent. The bigger towns like Fort Bragg and Eureka also boast antique shops, art galleries, theatres, live music shows and festivals.

Leave San Francisco on US 101 North, but stop just before the Golden Gate Bridge to sense the great natural and historic importance of the Golden Gate seaway which links the bays of San Francisco and San Pablo with the Pacific Ocean. The first ship here in historic times was the *San Carlos*, whose Spanish captain wrote in 1775 that the ocean's breach of the shoreline had created one of the finest natural harbours along the entire western coast of the Americas. A year later Spain built a presidio (fort) and a mission here, the beginnings of San Francisco. The seaway and the two large bays marked the northwest boundary of Spain's New World. The whole area remained a frontier until 1848 when the first specks of gold were found there, sparking the Gold Rush a year later. Since then millions of immigrants to America have sailed through this seaway and caught their first glimpse of the United States of America, which they believed was the great land of opportunity for the world's poor.

Continue for 5 miles along US 101 North, then a left turn for California 1, Tamalpais Valley and the Pacific coast. In just a little while, sidetrack off California 1 to visit Muir Woods NM. The access is awkward even now and

3

parking is limited, given the fact that each year a million people visit the two great groves of ancient coastal redwoods which are preserved and protected here for ever. In the mid-nineteenth century these magnificent trees were found in sheltered valleys along the whole length of the Pacific coast from Oregon to central California. By the turn of the century most had fallen to the logger's axe and the great redwoods faced extinction. The Bohemian and Cathedral Groves at Muir Woods NM were the last ones left in the entire area around San Francisco. President Theodore Roosevelt declared it a National Monument in 1908. Undoubtedly it is a hallowed place and one to be seen and savoured. The great trees pierce the blue sky. Short walks pass through cool, moist woodland dappled with sunshine and shade and alive with plants, animals and birds.

Coastal redwoods, Muir Woods NM

The monument is named for John Muir, one of America's greatest naturalists and conservationists. Muir emigrated from Scotland to America in 1848. For the rest of his life he devoted all his energies to understanding nature and pleading for its protection. Wild-looking, unkempt and a self-proclaimed tramp, he walked across huge tracts of America's wilderness, living off tea and bread and nature's bounty. He climbed mountains in deep snow and clambered to the tops of tall trees and waterfalls so that he could be more at one with nature. The wilderness was his university and he believed that nature was essential to the all-round well-being of people. His writings were hugely informed, philosophic and poetic, and grounded in what nature had taught him. He became a leading figure in the fight to conserve America's natural heritage and his work inspired such influential men as Theodore Roosevelt and the poet Ralph Waldorf Emerson. Muir's name and work still inspire the NPS and many Americans today. In California his name honours more natural places than anyone else's.

John Muir *(Image, Courtesy of the NPS. John Muir National Historic Site, Catalogue No. JOMU 4880 (El - 21))*

5

Point Reyes NS was created in 1962 to save a priceless piece of the nation's natural and cultural heritage which otherwise would have been engulfed by the growth of San Francisco. Today it protects 1,000 species of plants and animals and it is a wonderful place to see whales, seals, sea lions, elk and seabirds. Thousands of people come here to catch sight of the grey whale migrations. Between December and February the whales swim south to their calving grounds in the warm bays and lagoons of Baja California. In March the bulls swim back to the cold waters off Alaska, the mothers and calves following in April. Point Reyes Lighthouse is the best place to see these wonderful spectacles.

This National Seashore is a geological frontier of world significance. It stands astride the infamous San Andreas Fault that stretches 800 miles south along the Californian coast to San Diego. Below your feet two huge tectonic plates rub together, the Pacific Plate edging northwest about 2 inches a year and the North American Plate creeping westwards even more slowly. This area was the epicentre of the earthquake which destroyed much of San Francisco in 1906 and shifted Point Reyes Peninsula about 20 feet to the northwest. In the last 30 million years similar earthquakes have moved the peninsula 280 miles north from its original site near Los Angeles to where it is now. Test your confidence and nerves by walking the short self-guided Earthquake Trail near the Bear Valley Visitor Centre.

The peninsula has a fascinating human history. The Miwok village Kule Loklo near Bear Valley Visitor Centre provides some insights into Indian life here over the last 4,000 years. At Drakes Estero you can see the place where Francis Drake stopped for five weeks in 1579 to repair the *Golden Hind* during his voyage round the world. Redwoods were used to do some of his repairs, making the English the first white people to cut down some of these mammoth trees. The Miwoks helped to feed Drake's men while they were ashore and probably helped the sailors to cut down the redwoods. The ranches on the low-lying grasslands west of Inverness ridge stem from the days of the Gold Rush when they were set up to provide food for the mining towns and camps. Pierce Ranch, now restored, was built in 1858 and was a leading dairy ranch of its time. It is well worth a visit. Some half a dozen other ranches still function on the peninsula.

The highlight of my day was the visit to the lighthouse. It was misty and there was a cold wind blowing from the sea. It felt a bit like the North Yorkshire moors. From the car park it is a half-mile climb up a stony path to the cliff top where leaning cypress trees cling on stubbornly against strong ocean winds. Then come some 300 steps down a cliff to a small visitor centre and the lighthouse itself. The lighthouse is low down on the cliffs to help ships see its beacon blinking beneath the fog banks that bedevil this coast.

The eeriness was compounded by the mournful monotone sounds of the lighthouse's horn. Meanwhile, the lady on duty at the visitor centre waxed lyrical about Drake's circumnavigation of the world and his luck on a foggy day in finding the beach here to mend his sinking ship. I overheard her say to another visitor that her family was descended from Sir John Hawkins. What an extraordinary coincidence: a descendant of Hawkins talking here about Drake, two of the key figures in the defeat of the Spanish Armada when it attacked England in 1588! After this came a breathless and testing slog back up the 300 steps (it felt like 600) and down the trail to the car. A great experience!

Point Reyes Lighthouse

Just away from the coast, Petaluma is one of the best-preserved towns in California. Miraculously it was untouched by the earthquake in 1906. It has an historic riverfront, a town centre with many original buildings and some striking Victorian homes just beyond the main streets. These locations have featured in a whole host of Hollywood films, including *American Graffiti*, *Basic Instinct*, *The Horse Whisperer* and *True Crime*. It is a good place to stay overnight if coastal accommodations are full or too expensive.

The coastline north of Jenner is stunning. Near this small town the Russian River flows into the Pacific. California 1 turns inland to cross the estuary and then returns to the coastline to ride along narrow ledges on the steep side of the Coast Ranges. It is worth several stops at the parking spots to enjoy the great views to the south.

North California coast, near Jenner

Another stop worth making is Fort Ross SHP. The restored stockade is impressive, a huge rectangle of strongly timbered walls and gates with corner turrets overlooked by huge eucalyptus trees and standing on a large grassy ledge protruding out towards the sea. Built by the Russians in 1812, it has a commandant's house with exhibits of the occupation, and a Russian Orthodox chapel. For several decades the Russian presence here was a strong one. At a time when other nations also plied their trade and hunted sea mammals along this coast, the Russians had their own port (at Bodega Bay), three farms in the Coast Ranges, and Fort Ross. Officials of the Russian-American Company lived inside the fort, but about 250 Russians, Alaskans, Indians and Creoles (people of Russian descent married to these other peoples) lived outside the stockade. Food, furs, ships and timber were sent to Russian Alaska. Fort Ross had windmills, boatyards, a sandy cove, a blacksmith's shop and forge, and a cooperage. It was the site of the first commercial logging and shipbuilding in northern California. Alaskans in their fast, manoeuvrable kayaks proved very adept at killing sea otters and fur seals. But farming was always hard and sea otters and fur seals along the coast were hunted almost to extinction.

Fort Ross

The Russians left in 1841 and the fort passed into the hands of John Sutter, who was trying to build his own timber empire. Sutter took down the fort's buildings and shipped the planks southwards. Only a few years later Sutter opened a new sawmill at Coloma, where his business partner found gold in the mill race in 1848. The Gold Rush was on. Sutter's workers deserted the mill and his enterprise collapsed. How ironic! The next fifty years proved that there was a lot more money to be made in California from timber than from gold.

Mendocino is interesting to see, and not simply because of its Hollywood connection with *Murder She Wrote*. Call in at the Ford House Visitor Centre for an unexpected but fascinating insight into the logging industry in northern California during the second part of the nineteenth century. The Californian Gold Rush and the building of the Central Pacific Railroad in the 1860s created an insatiable demand for timber. The height and girths of the redwoods, their resistance to rot and their excellence for building construction and railway sleepers made them a lucrative prize for the loggers.

Ford House Visitor Centre incorporates the plain, unpretentious home built in 1852 by Jerome Bursley Ford, who supplied timber to San Francisco and the towns and camps of the goldfields further south.

One of the rooms has little gems of dioramas made up of small wood carvings and mounted photocopies of old photographs of uncertain origin that tell something of the story of Mendocino's role in this rapidly expanding activity in the 1850s.

The redwoods were taken down by hardy, resilient men, some of whom were disillusioned gold-diggers. Working in pairs, they stood facing each other on springboards at either side of the tree. They took a week or so to fell one tree and prepare it for haulage to the streams by ox-teams working on roads made of split logs. But American ingenuity thrived on practical problems and within a few years steam donkeys were used to haul logs to the watersides, streams were dammed to ensure the presence of water in winter, log flumes were invented, and steam paddleboats pulled logs 50 miles to the sawmills.

Schooners connected the coastal sawmills to the markets further south. Like some other places, Mendocino was a 'dog-hole port' – small, wave-lashed and, as the saying went, 'hard for even a dog to turn round in'. Ships went aground often. Chutes and cables were used to lower timber from the headland, the sailors steadying it by hand as the wood was stored on board ship. It was easy when the sea was calm, but highly dangerous when the weather was rough.

Images of the nineteenth-century logging industry, Mendocino *(Images of Bull Team Model and Saw published courtesy of California State Parks 2011. The images of schooners are old photographs whose origins are unclear, and copyright unknown)*

Fort Bragg, with its headlands and beaches, proves a good overnight stop. Shops with Western-style fronts line its Main Street. A bustling fishing harbour offers boat hire and whale-watching cruises; the North Coast Brewing Company has daily tours and a good restaurant; the colourful Mendocino Coast Botanical Gardens have an ocean backdrop; and the 'Skunk Train', billed as the most popular attraction on the northern coast, explores 40 miles of canyons, redwood groves, mountains and meadows.

Rockport to Eureka (c. 110 miles)

About 30 miles north of Fort Bragg, California 1 loses its purpose and identity, forced inland by the King Range which rises abruptly from the ocean with sides so steep and rugged that road engineers choose to avoid them. Just north of Rockport, the Shoreline Highway disappears through a deep cleft in the Coast Ranges and rides uphill through dense pine forests on a very serpentine and narrow road for 15 miles to the small town of Leggatt. Here it links with US 101, the 'Redwood Highway', mainly a freeway, which avoids the coast and penetrates some of northern California's best redwood country as it heads for the town of Eureka.

The great block of land avoided by these two roads is known as 'The Lost Coast'. Within this large area is the King Range NCA, a remote and pristine coastal wilderness hard to access and a paradise for lovers of nature and wildlife. Clothed in Douglas fir, the area is the home of black bears, mountain lions, elk, deer, coyotes, skunks, racoons and hundreds of species of birds, including bald eagles and falcons. At Garberville, 25 miles north of Leggatt on US 101, take the Redway turn and then head southwest to Shelter Cove. Here there is a wonderful stretch of coast with tidal pools, black sand beaches, harbour seals and sea lions. There are many foot trails and it is all a great mini-adventure! However, take care. Get trail maps and tide tables from the King Range Project Office, 786 Shelter Cove Road, Whitethorn – a left turn just before Shelter Cove.

Back on US 101 North, the freeway continues to Phillipsville, the beginning of an outstanding attraction known as the 'Avenue of the Giants'. The 'Avenue' runs close to US 101 for 32 miles. In the past it was a stagecoach dirt road to the gold mines of northern California and later on part of a road linking San Francisco to Eureka. The little towns along it, once logging camps and then tourist stops for early motorists, still retain features of these early days. The Riverhead Inn at Phillipsville was once the most famous roadhouse on this route. It is still open. So are the Miranda Garden Resort with its rental cabins in the redwoods and the Myers Country Inn, 130 years old, a stage-coach stop and one used by the author Jack London, who travelled this road regularly while researching his stories of the old frontier.

Myer's Country Inn at Myer's Flat, 'Avenue of the Giants'

The 'Avenue' is lined with tall redwoods and touches the eastern side of Humboldt Redwoods SP. It is an ideal place to see the awe-inspiring magnif-icence and majesty of the coastal redwoods, the monarchs of all America's forests. In Founder's Grove a former world champion tree known as the Dyerville Giant once stood 362 feet high with a girth of 17 feet. It was about 1,600 years old. It now lies flat on the ground, felled by other redwoods tum-bling down during heavy rains in 1991. But its usefulness is not over. Fallen redwoods lie on the ground for hundreds of years. They are the host, home and food supply for over 4,000 kinds of plants and animals, which in turn help to sustain the healthy life of the old forest. The grove has a lovely foot trail which winds through the trees, with sun shining through the canopy, and grass, ferns and wildflowers covering parts of the forest floor.

Just beyond Founder's Grove is Rockefeller Forest, the largest remaining old-growth redwood forest in the world. At its heart is a grove of trees which includes specimens to rival the Dyerville Giant. Giant Tree stands at 363 feet high, and Tall Tree reaches 359 feet. Trees stand closer, many lie rotting on

'Avenue of the Giants'

the ground. Moss, vines and creepers stifle grass and flowers. The canopy blots out the sun and the surroundings become a little oppressive and a bit scary! (The tallest redwood today is 379 feet and stands in Redwood NP, 80 miles north of Eureka. It is the tallest living thing in the world.)

Coastal redwoods were lost almost completely to loggers. In 1848 they occupied 2 million acres in California and Oregon; by 1900 only 4% of the trees were left standing. Founder's Grove commemorates the founders of the Save-the-Redwoods League, set up in 1917 to protect the remaining redwoods. Since then the League has spent millions of dollars to protect 170,000 acres of redwood trees in California, including the sequoia redwoods of the Sierra Nevada which had suffered a similar fate.

As always when in federal or state parks, look in at the Visitor Centre. The exhibit concerning Charles Kellogg and his Travel Log is fascinating.

Like John Muir, Kellogg was a creature of the wilderness, tramping through the forests of America, Europe and the Tropics. Amongst his many achievements he sang bird songs, recording them for the Victor Talking Machine Company. He also starred in vaudeville shows all over North America, and once sang to an audience of 20,000 people at London's Crystal Palace.

One of Kellogg's great ambitions was to 'awaken interest in the great redwood forests of California and help in their preservation'. To serve this lifelong passion, he single-handedly fashioned with axe and adze a mobile home from a 6-ton section of a fallen redwood tree. Its accommodation featured kitchenette, dining table, stove, folding double bed, bookcase, dresser, electric lights, toilet, running water, and a single room for a guest. He rubbed 12 pounds of beeswax by hand into the wood, giving it a natural rich red rose colour. He mounted his home on a lorry chassis, powered by a Nash-Quad engine with four-wheel drive. Then he completed four successful tours of America, first to sell Liberty Bonds for the federal government to help it win the First World War, and then to spread his message about the plight of the redwoods. In pristine condition, the Travel Log remains a popular attraction in the Visitor Centre. Imagine driving this extraordinary vehicle for thousands of miles across mountains, deserts and plains on the dirt roads of a century ago!

The Nash-Quad Travel Log: exterior and interior *(Permission to photograph these images by courtesy of the Visitor Centre, Humboldt Redwoods SP, California)*

Continue north along the 'Avenue' and rejoin US 101 just past Pepperwood. The next settlement is Scotia, still a logging company town. The mill complex stands on a great bend of the Eel River, the company's houses for retirees and workers above it on the wooded valley side. Ownership of these properties today rests with the Humboldt Redwood Company which works 328 miles of coastal forest, preserving all old-growth trees growing before 1800 with girths of 4 feet or more.

Just north of Scotia on US 101, take the Grizzly Bluff Road to the village of Ferndale. A dairy town since the late nineteenth century, this is a remarkable place. The central square mile of the village is full of Victorian houses and other buildings and it is a California Historical Landmark. The quaint main street with its late-nineteenth-century buildings painted in white, pink, yellow and purple reminded me of Bermuda. It well deserves its listing on the National Register of Historic Places. Hollywood films have been made here. A pastoral idyll, this is most definitely worth the short detour from US 101 before making for Eureka.

Eureka also has a fine historic old town centre. The Old Town is well restored with scores of elegant Victorian homes built in the days when timber was king. Pre-eminent is the house built in the 1880s by William Carson, a

Carson House, Eureka

multi-millionaire in the logging business. An incredible model of conspicuous consumption, his redwood house was built in a most exuberant style with money no object. A hundred craftsmen were employed to fashion the house both outside and inside. The Ford House in Mendocino is extremely humble and modest in comparison.

Restoration work in the town remains ongoing. The town's Boardwalk has fine water views and the century-old *MV Madaket* provides cruises around Humboldt Bay. The Samoa Cookhouse, said to be the last surviving cookhouse in the West, boasts meals fit for lumberjacks. Fort Humboldt SP has good museums about the logging industry and the history of the area.

Eureka to Lassen Volcanic NP (c. 200 miles)

CAUTION

The roads between Eureka and Lassen Volcanic NP suffer bad weather in winter. The state of the roads and their driveability can be checked at any time by phoning CALTRANS 1-800-427-7623. Say or press the road number and listen to the current conditions there. If this drive is not feasible, take California 101 South to Santa Rosa and then California 12 to Sonoma.

Lassen Volcanic NP is open all year, weather permitting. However, the main road through the park between the Northwest and Southwest Entrance Stations is snowbound for about nine months of the year, the time of opening perhaps as late as early July. This information can be obtained by ringing the park on 530-595-4480. If the main road is closed, a decision has to be made about which entrance to use. The advice below may help you to decide. To try to drive from one entrance to the other using minor lower roads outside the park is time-consuming and difficult.

ADVICE

Redding and Red Bluff are both about 50 miles from the park and there is a good choice of motels in both towns. My best advice is to stop in Redding overnight, drive through the park from north to south and then stay the next night in Red Bluff. Altogether the round trip is no more than 150 miles and you have sufficient time to spend in the park itself.

From Eureka, go 8 miles north on US 101 and then head east to Redding on California 299. Most of this two-lane winding and undulating road is a Scenic Highway. It crosses the Coast Ranges, travels for miles along the very picturesque valley of the wild Trinity River where miners once dug for gold, and offers splendid views of both the Trinity Mountains and Whiskeytown Lake.

The great mountains and forests seen on this drive were also part of the great timber bonanza of the nineteenth and twentieth centuries. The predominant tree was the Douglas fir, named for David Douglas, a Scot sent to the American Northwest by the Royal Horticultural Society in 1823 to study the forests of the region. The Douglas fir lacked the height of a coastal redwood, but nevertheless it was another great prize for the lumbermen. With a girth of 12 feet, a trunk free of branches for the first 100 feet, and wood tough and straight-grained, it was ideal for use as masts, beams and spars, and as supports for bridges and large buildings.

There is no doubt who was the most famous pioneer logger in the American forests in the nineteenth century. He was the fictional Paul Bunyan, whose name still echoes in the towns and streets of northern California. Hugely mythologised and revered, he was talked about in every logger's bunkhouse where his reputation and exploits were embroidered and exaggerated every time his story was told.

Said to be born in the east, Paul Bunyan, accompanied by his lifelong companion the mighty blue ox called Babe, worked his way west cutting down the great forests of the country. He was a superman, a hulking giant who parted his hair with a broadaxe and pulled up pine trees to comb his beard with their roots. He chopped down trees with a four-bladed axe and removed whole sections of forest with his great timber scythe or three-mile-wide crosscut saw. Once, thinking that Babe was dead, he dug a grave which later filled with water and was called the Puget Sound. The earth and rocks he threw up to make it became the Cascade Mountains. He even made the Grand Canyon! No job was too big and no hazard too great for him. And if the tools were no good, then he invented new ones. Paul Bunyan imbued the loggers with the spirit, will and determination to do their work, especially in the far west where the redwoods and the Douglas fir were the biggest trees they had ever seen. They were the last great work of Paul Bunyan and Babe. Afterwards they retired to Alaska and were never heard of again, except in the tall tales of the earthly loggers they left behind.

Lassen Volcanic NP is another excellent drive. It is the highest road in the Cascade Mountains, rising through many steep bends and crossing the snow-line to give some wonderful vistas of a primeval volcanic wilderness, hardly touched by humans, and another example of an area saved from the logger's axe by the federal government. The park is one of northern California's biggest areas of old-growth forest. Including the recommended stops, the 30-mile drive takes between three and four hours.

From Redding take US 44 to the Northwest Entrance of the park and then follow the main road all the way to the Southwest exit. I stopped at the Kohm Yah-mah-nee Visitor Centre to watch an introductory film about the park. I liked its beginning. In this land of fire and smoke the ancient Indians imagined the rise of a great mountain which brought warmth and fertility to a first world of cold and inhospitable water and flood. The great mountain was the source of life and a symbol of the great power of nature. For the Indians who still live here, the mountain is sacred and central to their spiritual life.

As the drive begins, Manzanita Lake is to the right and Reflection Lake to the left, both with short and easy walking trails. Black bears sometimes wander there. Reflection Lake mirrors Lassen Peak and attracts photographers. Loomis Museum holds excellent artefacts and photographs of the volcanic eruptions in the park between 1914 and 1921. Chaos Jumbles, a scene of large jagged rocks, was caused by a violent rockslide from Chaos Crags some 300 years ago. Beyond here the road coincides briefly with the Nobles Trail, one of the rugged wagon trails used in the 1850s and 1860s by pioneers coming west to Redding and Shasta after leaving the main part of the California Trail. The park takes its name from Peter Lassen, like Nobles a great promoter of northern California, who had blazed a wagon trail here a few years earlier than his contemporary.

Mount Lassen from Manzanita Lake, Lassen Volcanic NP

The biggest eruption in the park occurred in 1915. The road between Crags and Summit Lake still has clear signs of the devastation caused by the exploding volcano. Fire, lava and mud stripped this area of all vegetation in a path of destruction between 2 and 3 miles wide. Summit Lake is at 7,000 feet, but the road continues upwards to 8,512 feet, winding round Lassen Peak as it does so. This mountain is a volcanic vent of Brokeoff Volcano, an eroded mountain to the southwest.

Dropping down from the high ground, the sights, sounds and smells of the park undergo a distinct change. Bumpass Hell is a place of rising clouds of steam, boiling springs, bubbling mud and the strong smell of sulphur. Big Boiler hisses water as hot as 275 degrees Fahrenheit. To see it up close you have to get out of your car, hold your nose and follow the walking trail over rocky ground for one and a half miles to a long boardwalk which loops round the active hydrothermal basin. The ground beneath belies its look of firmness. A Dutchman called Kendall Vanhook Bumpass once fell through it and burned one leg so badly in the boiling mud and water below that he had to have it amputated. When I was there in June 2010, snow had destroyed the walkway and it was closed to the public. But there are grand vistas even from the Bumpass Hell car park.

Bumpass Hell, Lassen Volcanic NP *(Images of Bumpass Hell and mudpot (inset) provided by Lassen Volcanic NP, courtesy of the NPS)*

More lovely vistas follow as the road continues downwards to Little Hot Springs Valley and the Sulphur Works, also areas of hydrothermal activity. Remember Bumpass, however, and keep to the proper trails. I was told that one of the places of hydrothermal activity in the park is called Fart Gulch. I was too coy to ask a ranger its whereabouts and I could not see it on a map. I kept looking, but I never got sight, sound or smell of it. But several places strongly assail the senses and would easily qualify for the name!

Road between Bumpass Hell and Sulphur Works

Sulphur Works

Lassen Volcanic NP to Sonoma and the Wine Country (c. 225 miles)

Leave the park on California 89 and then turn west on California 66 to Red Bluff. Then head south on I-5 to Williams, west on California 20, south on California 29 through Clearlake and then go west to Sonoma, just past Rutherford.

The 'Wine Country' occupies an area of about 7,000 square miles, spreading along the sheltered valleys of the Napa and Russian rivers in the Coast Ranges immediately north of San Francisco Bay. Green pinstripe vineyards stand below hills covered in oak and grass. The ocean keeps winters mild, foggy air cools the summer heat, and bright early autumn sunshine ripens the grapes. Some 300 wineries make 2 billion bottles of wine a year, including Cabernet Sauvignon, Chardonnay, Chenin Blanc, Merlot, Pinot Noir, Sauvignon Blanc and Zinfandel. They offer endless opportunities to taste and buy wine and they have become major players in the world's wine markets.

This drive ends in Sonoma, partly because I love its warm ambience, partly because its background fits well with the themes of this book, and partly because Sonoma claims a special place in the history of wine-making.

Sonoma was the site of the last of the 21 Spanish missions to be built in California (in 1823). It was secularised in 1834 by the Mexican government, but served for a while as a bastion against Russian and American infiltrators into the area. The military commissioner General Mariano Vallejo brought in his own Mexican settlers, built up Sonoma's army garrison and created a central plaza in the traditional Spanish style. He also absorbed the mission lands into his own estates and employed the Indians who lived there. In 1846 war broke out between America and Mexico. Groups of American settlers already in the area took advantage and seized Sonoma, imprisoning Vallejo. They raised a flag depicting a bear and proclaimed Sonoma the capital of an independent 'California Republic'. This flag is now California's state flag.

Today Sonoma retains its Hispanic origins. It is not Main Street America. Sonoma SHP stands on the old mission site with its restored church. It protects the town's historic buildings, including the old Mexican two-storey adobe barracks and Vallejo's attractive home furnished in the style of the mid-nineteenth century. The walk to his house is through meadows full of wildflowers and blackbirds with red wings rivalling one another for territory. The plaza area, once the scene of drills, parades and fiestas, is now a lovely and spacious green area with trees and plants. The Visitor Centre in the town square has good information about wineries and other places to visit in the Sonoma Valley.

Vallejo's House, Sonoma

Sonoma has a special place in the history of wine-making. Its old mission planted the first vineyards in northern California, the wine used in the Catholic mass. Bueno Vista is the state's oldest commercial winery. Its creator was Agoston Haraszthy, a Hungarian aristocrat, said to be the founder of the Californian wine industry.

Haraszthy led a remarkable life in America, his business ventures full of ups and downs and his activities varied in the extreme. Before reaching southern California as the master of his own wagon train, he had grown grapes, raised sheep and pigs, operated a ferry and had business interests in a brickyard, a sawmill, a general store and a hotel in Wisconsin. In California he was a sheriff, a US marshall, an assayer and a refiner of gold, and a state assemblyman. He tried to grow grapes again. His life took its final turn in the early 1850s when he tasted wine made from grapes grown on Vallejo's estates in Sonoma. He moved to Sonoma, convinced that this was the place to fulfil his dream of making the best wines in the world. In 1857 he produced a new variety of wine called Zinfandel.

Sonoma is a good centre for local touring by car. Drives can be made along the lower Napa Valley, also very famous as a wine producing area, and to other State Parks, for example, the Jack London SHP. Sonoma is about 50 miles from San Francisco and the airport. The road leads back across the Golden Gate Bridge and, by following US 101 the chance to see more of the Golden Gate area including the impressive area of the Presidio where Spain built a strong fort to defend its American interests from other European powers after 1750. From 1848 the presidio was then occupied by the Americans as a military base until very recent times.

Buena Vista Winery, Sonoma

2

Missions and Parks

Central California

This drive begins in Santa Monica on the western side of Los Angeles. It uses California 1 and US 101 to explore the coastline and Coast Ranges as far north as Monterey Bay. There are many stunning human and physical landscapes such as Santa Barbara, Hearst Castle, Big Sur and the Monterey Peninsula. Everywhere Spanish place names indicate California's rich Hispanic heritage. Ten of the 21 missions built by the Spanish Crown in California were founded in this central part of the state. Monterey was the capital of Spanish and Mexican California until 1848. Many Spanish and Mexican buildings are protected sites in several of California's excellent state parks and museums.

From Monterey Bay the drive continues eastwards across California's Central Valley and San Joaquin River to the western flanks of the Sierra Nevada. In the late 1860s John Muir walked across this very piece of the Central Valley, enthralled by its wild, fragrant and abundant plants and animals. He said the whole area was a bee garden of lavish richness. Today, this hugely productive farming area is one of America's premier food baskets, its crops and livestock in farms, vineyards and ranches further echoing the state's legacy from the Spanish missions.

The final part of the drive goes through two highly impressive National Parks – Yosemite and Sequoia/Kings Canyon. They protect a very large portion of mountain and forest wilderness in the mighty Sierra Nevada, a name meaning 'Snowy Range' and given to the area by an eighteenth-century Spanish missionary.

Suggested start/finish:	Los Angeles
Length of journey:	About 1,000 miles; 8 to 10 days
Best time of year:	All year round along the coast
	Summer weekdays in the Sierra NPs – all roads open.
	The main road in each park is open all year, and
	Yosemite Valley, Grant Grove and Giant Forest are

25

Weather:

accessible but chains may be needed in bad weather.
The coast from Los Angeles to Point Conception enjoys
a Mediterranean-type climate.

Point Conception to Monterey Bay has fair sunny days
all year round, with occasional winter rain.

Fog is common from July to the end of September.

Yosemite Valley (4,000 feet) has warm, dry summers
and cool winters.

Grant Grove to Giant Forest (5,000–7,000 feet) has
warm summer days but cool nights, and cold winters
with snow.

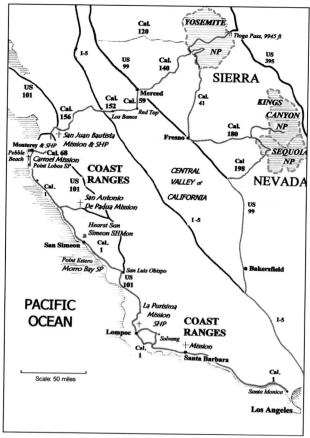

Map 3: Central California

THE BROWN ROBES OF EL CAMINO REAL

Twenty-one Spanish missions were built in the Californian wilderness between 1769 and 1823. They formed a chain some 650 miles long from San Diego to San Francisco. The missions were run by brown-robed Franciscan friars. Spanish settlements grew up around most of the missions and four presidios (forts) were built to guard them from attacks by foreign nations and hostile Indians. The presidios were at San Diego, Santa Barbara, Monterey and San Francisco.

The missionaries worked to save the souls of the Indians, convert them to the Roman Catholic faith and make them good, loyal citizens of the Spanish Crown. Each mission had its white adobe church, usually brightly painted inside, lit with candles and full of Catholic images. Mass was celebrated every day and the church bell governed the daily rhythm of work and prayer. Shaded cloisters, patios, gardens and fountains, usually within a quadrangle of buildings which included the church and only one door to the outside, created an atmosphere of permanence, safety, peace and tranquillity for both the missionaries and the Indians.

Each mission strove to be self-sufficient, but the friars traded with sea captains along the coast for things like tools, furniture, glass, hardware, cloth, pots and pans, and musical instruments. Just before the Mexican Revolution it is calculated that collectively the missions produced 123,000 bushels of grain a year and owned 396,000 cattle, 62,000 horses and 321,000 pigs, sheep and goats. Some 100,000 Indians were said to be Christianised (called 'neophyte' Indians).

Statue of a Franciscan padre

The Mexican Revolution changed everything. In 1834 the missions were secularised and their buildings, land and livestock sold off for paltry sums to farmers and ranchers. Most churches were abandoned and fell victim to vandals, the weather and earthquakes. After 1848, when California became part of the USA, the Catholic Church in America gained ownership of the mission church buildings under federal legislation passed in the presidencies of James Buchanan and Abraham Lincoln. Today, four of them are run by Franciscans, but all have been restored or rebuilt and nearly all of them are now active churches for the parishes they serve.

Historians both praise and condemn the defunct mission system, but the old mission churches are a growing tourist attraction. They provide a unique glimpse of California's Spanish roots, possessing as they do many architectural and artistic treasures which surprise many visitors to the Southwest. They have left an indelible mark on present-day California in other ways too, including a very considerable number of Hispanic people who still speak Spanish and are Roman Catholic; widespread livestock and farming activities; a love of cowboys, horses and rodeos; and Hispanic cuisine and social customs.

Drive highlights

US 101 and California 1

US 101 follows much of the old route known as El Camino Real ('The Royal Road'). In the late eighteenth century this was a narrow but well-travelled dirt road linking all of Spain's Californian missions. Today the road is marked by a fast freeway, US 101, through the oak-studded, verdant Coast Ranges. California 1 was the state's first public highway, built about a century ago. A slow, narrow highway, it hugs a dramatic shoreline of rugged cliffs and headlands, dunes, beaches and coves, river estuaries and wetlands. It is congested in summer and during weekends and public holidays. Occasionally the two roads join into one.

Santa Monica (Los Angeles) to Santa Barbara (c. 75 miles)

Drive west from Santa Monica on California 1 to Oxnard and then join US 101 for Santa Barbara. The state highway follows the base of the Santa Monica Mountains. It gives great views of the Malibu Pier and Surf-Rider Beach and a wonderful panorama of the mountains, the bay and the offshore Channel Islands NP. This park protects the peaks of sunken mountains which are the sanctuary for birds, seals, sea lions, dolphins and whales.

Santa Barbara basks in a Mediterranean-type climate. The town centre gleams with whitewashed buildings, red tiles, orange trees and lovely bougainvilleas. Its main civic building is the County Courthouse, built in Spanish-Moorish style after an earthquake destroyed the town in 1925. But Santa Barbara's roots go much deeper. Its presidio and mission church loudly proclaim its origins in old Spanish California.

The presidio is the only one of the four Spanish forts built in California to remain standing. One of its buildings, El Cuartel, is the oldest in the town and the second oldest in California. Built in 1782, the fort was the military and political centre for all the lands between Los Angeles and San Luis Obispo. Interestingly, the first soldiers here were a mix of Spaniards, Mexican Indians, Sephardic Jews and Africans, some of whom married local Chumash Indians. Many present-day people in Santa Barbara trace their ancestry back to these first military occupiers. The fort had a chapel, a padre's room, living quarters for officers and married men, barracks and a store. Old soldiers re-tired here, building adobe houses and adding to the town's Spanish life and culture.

Santa Barbara Mission was the tenth to be built and it was dedicated in 1786. Its elevated and well-watered site looks out over the fort, oak trees and the ocean. The mission's original water supply remains visible even today. A stream above the site was dammed, the water falling along a stone aqueduct to a settling basin and then a reservoir near the church. The reservoir fed the fountain, orchards and gardens. Overflow from the Moorish fountain built in 1808 supplied a laundry basin where Indian women did the washing.

The mission church is most impressive and in much better physical condition than any other in central California. It is the fourth one to be built here and is said to be one of the most photographed buildings in America. Known as the 'Queen of the Missions', its imposing façade includes

Santa Barbara Presidio

Santa Barbara Mission Church

Moorish-style towers and a Roman-style doorway topped by four statues – Faith, Hope, Charity and Santa Barbara. The church interior, with its rich collections of reredos, statues and paintings, remains much as it was in 1820. The mission has functioned since 1786 hardly without interruption. Soaked in tradition, it has always been a prestigious and dominant force in local life and its brown-robed friars continue to play a leading role in civic affairs. It is also a theological seminary, an archive for a vast collection of documents of Franciscan activities throughout the American West, a retreat for individuals who seek respite from the pressures of the world and feel the need for spiritual guidance, and a tourist venue for millions of people.

Santa Barbara to San Simeon (c. 170 miles)

Continue on US 101 along the coast to Las Cruces, turning northwards into the lush wine country of the Santa Inez valley and the hugely popular town of Solvang, built in traditional Danish style. If you can park, this is definitely worth a stretch of the legs. Afterwards, drive to Lompoc along the country road California 246, or go back to Las Cruces and go north to Lompoc on California 1, its fields ablaze with flowers from May to September. I stayed here to visit La Purisma Mission the next day.

La Purisima Mission SHP is two miles northeast of Lompoc. Founded in 1787, this was the eleventh mission. It flourished for 24 years, was largely demolished in 1812 by a huge earthquake, and was then rebuilt to enjoy a second period of prosperity. At that time the mission occupied 300,000 acres, protected 1,000 Chumash Indians and ran a huge ranching enterprise with over 20,000 cattle, sheep and other livestock. After secularisation, however, the mission gradually became a ruin. A century later the NPS and the New Deal's Civilian Conservation Corps used original tools to restore the mission buildings and refurbish them to their condition in 1820. La Purisima gives a wonderful chance to see how missions worked two centuries ago.

El Camino Real went directly to the mission door, its line marked by a footpath which visitors still use. Two of the original bells still hang in the belfry, one made of wood, its bronze replacement never purchased for lack of funds. Candles flicker in the dark church interior with its oil paintings, pictures of the Stations of the Cross and uneven floor of terracotta tiles. The frugally furnished padre's room and guest quarters have bare floors, the odd carpet or rug and simple hand-made wooden furniture. In the guardroom, once occupied by five soldiers, leather jackets and shields made from animal hides hang against a wall. Lances, swords and flintlock muskets are stacked up in a corner. Canvas and wooden beds, a dining table with wooden plates and earthenware jugs, and a card table fill out the room. There are many

The frugality of the missions *(Permission for the use of these author's images given by La Purisima Mission SHP, California State Parks 2011)*

work areas – the soap and tallow vats; the olive press; the pottery, blacksmith, carpentry and weaving workshops; the granary and the community kitchen; the gardens and animal enclosures. The cattle and sheep in these enclosures today are descendants of the animals brought to the New World by the Spanish. Self-sufficiency was at the heart of the mission's daily life. There is also a hospital which cared for sick and dying Indians whose resistance to European diseases was low. Girls and unmarried young women were housed in a separate building, the monjerio, where they learned to cook and sew. They were locked in at night.

The next morning I made an early start, driving north on California 1 and US 101 to make the time for an afternoon visit to Hearst Castle at San Simeon. Morro Bay SP has a good Museum of Natural History, including a Chumash garden which shows how these Indians used plants in their everyday lives. The coast at Estero Bluffs SP, with its cliffs, coastal terraces, sea stacks, small estuaries, wetlands, freshwater marshes and abundant wildlife probably still looks as it did when Spanish sailors saw it four centuries ago.

Hearst Castle was the home of the multi-millionaire newspaper mogul William Randolph Hearst. Now it is a California State Historical Monument. No greater contrast to the plain, simple, straightforward, make-do-and-mend frontier missions could be imagined. The extravagance and splendour of 'The Enchanted Hill' built by an exceedingly rich man for his own pleasure during the lean years of the 1920s and 1930s when there was widespread poverty and hardship in America does not win the approval of some who visit it today. Nevertheless, it is a must-see attraction and an unforgettable experience! It is the most sumptuous expression of conspicuous consumption in the Southwest, made all the more remarkable when contrasted with the frugality of La Purisima Mission.

Hearst came from a fabulously wealthy background. His father made three fortunes, one in silver, the second in gold, the third in copper. In 1919 Hearst inherited 250,000 acres of land in San Simeon and Santa Rosa. Over the next 30 years he built on the high ground above the beach a lavish, no-expense-spared, private residential complex which contained his main house, Casa Grande, with imposing towers and balconies; three sumptuous guesthouses, Casa del Sol, Casa del Mare, and Casa del Monte; two huge swimming pools, one outdoors and one indoors; and all surrounded by shaded walkways, gardens, terraces and patios with extensive views across the sea and Coast Ranges. The main house contains 38 bedrooms and 41 bathrooms; the three guesthouses 18 bedrooms and 20 bathrooms. The architecture was inspired by Hearst's love of Greek, Roman and medieval buildings and the four houses are full of fabulous ceilings, furniture, paintings, tapestries, rugs and sculptures collected during his extensive and numerous tours in the Mediterranean area. Hearst's guests were the rich and the famous, people like Winston Churchill, Charles Lindbergh, Charlie Chaplin, Greta Garbo and Jean Harlow. Cary Grant drily remarked that this was a good place to spend the Great Depression.

The splendour of Hearst Castle (*Permission for the use of these author's images given by Hearst Castle, California State Parks, 2011*)

San Simeon to Monterey Bay (c. 140 miles)

Stay in San Simeon for the night, make another early start next day, and keep heading north. A few miles beyond Sand Dollar Beach is a small road (G14) to Jolon and Lockwood. It crosses the Santa Lucia Range and in about 20 miles reaches Mission San Antonio de Padua, nestled in the Valley of the Oaks on the eastern side of the mountains. The highest part of these mountains is named for Father Serra, who founded the mission. It became a wealthy one and there was a strong bond between the missionaries and the Indians. The soldiers, priests and settlers who founded San Francisco camped here on their way north in 1776. After secularisation, the Indians were driven into the mountains and the mission was abandoned. In 1903 the California Historic Landmarks League came to its rescue and restoration began. The Franciscans returned there in 1928. In 1948 the Hearst Foundation gave money to help with the rebuilding.

San Antonio de Padua Mission

Father John, who headed the mission when I visited it, told me that he had been one of the friars who had worked to restore the buildings. While we spoke his mind was partly on other matters, including the disarray in his office, a power cut and the whereabouts of his cat. St Francis loved all animals, and Father John certainly liked cats. The visiting electrician was doing his best to restore power, but the search for the cat was taking up too much time. In all of this domestic chaos the cat suddenly re-appeared. Its name was Haywire, an apt name in the circumstances. There was no doubt that Father John loved the mission. For him it had a special aura of peace and joy. He said the Indians felt the same way. They still hold some places in the valley sacred and they use the mission as their social centre. With its mountain backdrop and profusion of trees and meadows, the mission enjoys the rural serenity it has always possessed. It is a step back into the late eighteenth century and a lovely place to visit.

Now it's back to the coast and California 1, and north over Big Sur to Monterey. Take care! Mudslides and fog are potential hazards, but the visual rewards are great. This is the most scenic stretch on California 1, and for a short distance a wonderfully wild place free of roadside motels, fast-food restaurants and flashing neon. In places the road looks down a thousand feet to waves and surf crashing into bays and coves and wearing away the giant headlands. At Point Sur the automated lighthouse stands high on a volcanic rock, a wonderful land- and seascape.

Headlands at Big Sur

Point Lobos SP provides a good walking coastal trail. Breathe in the salt air and watch seabirds, seals, sea lions and sea otters. It is a gorgeous place.

One landscape artist said this was 'the greatest meeting of land and sea in the world' and many people think that this is the crown jewel in California's State Park system. The Spaniards called this place the Point of the Sea Wolves, because it rang with the cries of sea lions. The car park stands on the site of an old whaling station and a drawing on an information board shows the activities of the whalers there many years ago. Nearby is a large whaler's cabin, built with pine and redwood by some Chinese fishermen early in the 1850s. They were the first here, but Portuguese whalers came in later.

The Monterey Bay area (c. 50 miles)

This area deserves at least a two-night stop in Monterey to allow a full day to visit Carmel Mission, the area of Pebble Beach and the State Historic Park in Old Monterey.

Carmel Mission Church and quadrangle

The serene San Carlos Borromeo de Carmelo stands as the monument to Padre Juniper Serra who lived here between 1770 and 1784. Framed by sky and mountains, its façade includes a Moorish tower with nine bells and a star window over the main doorway. Exotic plants, fountains and statues crowd its garden and quadrangle. After secularisation the mission's lands were sold right up to the walls of the church, which soon fell into ruin. Today the church is one of the most authentic restorations of all the mission churches, its quadrangle a place of great peace and tranquillity.

Juniper Serra was a tiny man with an iron constitution. Born in Spain, he became the first Father-President of the Franciscan missions in California. He walked and rode mules over huge distances in the Californian wilderness looking for suitable mission sites, holding mass and baptising Indians as he went. Serra's restored cell at Carmel Mission reflects his humility and asceticism. The tiny room contains a single bed of wooden boards, a blanket, a table and chair, a chest, a candlestick and a gourd. Serra is buried at Carmel. Above his grave there is a finely sculptured sarcophagus depicting Serra surrounded by the figures of three other Franciscan padres who are also buried there.

From Carmel, go to Pebble Beach and take a toll-road drive around the Monterey Peninsula. Forest and dunes have been transformed by the Del

The iconic lone cypress, Pebble Beach, central California

Monte Corporation into a private and exclusive resort for multi-millionaires. This itself is a compelling attraction, but the hour-long 17-mile drive also includes great photographic opportunities and inspiring views of rocky shore-lines, beaches and surf, gently rolling hills, wildlife and unique landmarks like the Lone Cypress, a tree that has clung tenaciously to the bare granite cliffs here for more than two centuries. Praised by visitors over many years, it is revered for its stubborn longevity. The tree has become the iconic symbol of the Pebble Beach Company, which is dedicated to the conservation of this unique piece of the Californian coast.

Monterey has just cause to boast that it is the most historic city in California. It has proud beginnings. Its name first appeared in the records in 1602 when Sebastian Vizcaino landed here in his quest for safe harbours for Spanish galleons carrying wealth from the Philippines. The presidio was founded in 1770 when Father Serra dedicated California's second mission. (The church was moved to its present site in Carmel a year later.) Planting the seeds of a new colony was a colourful, very impressive and august occa-sion. A Spanish artist much later painted Serra standing under a large white cloth canopy below a tall, spreading tree. The makeshift altar also had a crucifix, silver candlesticks, a bell and a Bible. The sea captain and army commander were kneeling in front of Serra and behind them, in three sides of a square, were the soldiers and sailors in red jackets with white sashes, monks in their brown habits and nearly naked Indians. A three-masted galleon lay at anchor in the bay. Five years later, Monterey became the capital of Spanish California, a position it retained under Spanish and then Mexican rule until 1848.

To best explore Old Monterey, go to the Custom House Plaza, near Fish-erman's Wharf. The Plaza is California's oldest government building, collecting dues from ships when this town was Mexico's primary port of entry. America raised its flag here in 1846 during its two-year war with Mexico, adding 600,000 square miles of land to America in doing so. The Plaza's 7-acre site, the Monterey SHP, preserves the historical and architectural her-itage of Old Monterey. A free 2-mile walking tour of Old Monterey takes place every morning at 10.30, except Thursdays. The walk takes about 45 minutes but it is on a first-come-first-served basis. However, the Visitor Cen-tre near the Custom House has free maps and notes of the tour and it is easy to follow the route yourself without a guide. Just follow the gold stars stamped into the pavements and go at your own pace through the old town with its historic streets and adobe buildings. Among its many attractions are the Cooper-Molera Adobe and Gardens, Larkin House, the Royal Presidio

Chapel (which became California's first cathedral) and Colton Hall where, in 1849, the constitution of California was written. And when you have done the history bit there are excellent retreats at Fisherman's Wharf and the Monterey Bay Aquarium. A lovely old town with a wonderful ambience!

Customs House, Monterey SHP

Colton Hall, Monterey SHP

Monterey to Yosemite NP (c. 160 miles)

Leave Monterey on California 68 to Salinas, go north on US 101, and then east on California 156 towards Hollister. At San Juan Bautista the old mission stands in a small settlement whose central plaza is frozen in the nineteenth century. The town's plaza and the streets and buildings next to it form San Juan Bautista SHP. North of the plaza and next to the mission cemetery with its thousands of graves of Indian and Spanish people there is even an original piece of El Camino Real. Imagine this with padres, Indians, soldiers and tradesmen using it to walk to and from the mission and the town. Mission and park together embrace handsome old buildings, fascinating local history and little shops, boutiques and restaurants. The park has guided walking tours, but again maps are available and you can do your own thing if you wish

San Juan Bautista Mission and El Camino Real

Father Lasuen founded San Juan Bautista Mission in 1797. It was the fifteenth and the largest church in the Californian mission chain. The local Indians proved welcoming and loyal. The very colourful and striking reredos in the church was painted in 1818 by a Boston sailor said to be the first American settler in California. He had jumped ship and painted the murals in return for food and lodging. Right on the San Andreas Fault, the mission has periodically suffered serious earthquake damage. Today its buildings are reinforced with steel and concrete. When it was secularised in 1835, the mission's lands were divided by the administrator Jose Tiburcio Castro between his relatives, friends and neighbours and some of the Indians. Nevertheless, the church has always had a pastor and the congregation remains predominantly Spanish speaking.

Today life in San Juan Bautista is lived at a slow and steady pace. In the 1860s and 1870s it was a different story. The square bustled with freight wagons servicing local ranches and mines. Stagecoaches arrived and left almost every hour. Coach passengers were put up at the Plaza Hotel. Dancing, political rallies, temperance meetings and travelling shows took place on the second floor of Plaza Hall. The town even had its own famous outlaw, Tiburcio Vasquez, who helped himself to American property and evaded the clutches of law enforcement officers by hiding out amongst local Mexican families. The town's prosperity proved short-lived, however. The railway never came to San Juan Bautista and its heyday as a stagecoach hub and a trade and supply centre for the surrounding area ended. However, these various buildings, and others in nearby streets, remain as strong reminders of San Juan Bautista as it was in the later nineteenth century.

Castro House is interesting in its own right. It looks much the same now as when it was built. In 1848 it was purchased by the Breen family. Patrick Breen, his wife and seven children were survivors of the Donner Party tragedy on the California Trail in 1847 (see Chapter 4). Arriving destitute in the town, they were given free shelter in the mission. When the Gold Rush began, 16-year-old John Breen became a prospector and returned to his family with $10,000 of gold dust. The Breens bought Castro House and 400 acres of prime farming land in the San Juan Valley. The house remained in the family's possession until 1933, when it became part of the State Park. The Breens are remembered in the town as successful landowners, ranchers and attorneys. They lived the American dream.

Later in the day I drove on towards Yosemite NP. I stayed at Merced, made an early start next morning, spent much of the day touring Yosemite, and then drove to a motel in Fresno for the night. Yosemite itself has various types of accommodation – hotels, motels, cabins and tents – but it is not easy to find space at short notice in the summer. (The telephone number for the Yosemite Reservations Office is 801-559-5000.)

Yosemite NP blows your mind away. It is the grand centrepiece of the Sierra Nevada, a vast, thickly forested wilderness of glaciated alpine mountains, massive granite formations, wild river valleys, spectacular waterfalls and lakes, stands of giant trees, open meadows with wildflowers and butterflies, and large animals like black bears, mountain lions and mule deer. John Muir said it was 'the grandest of all the special temples of Nature I was ever permitted to enter'. It is one of America's very best and most popular National Parks.

Yosemite Valley and Mariposa Grove have been protected by the federal government since 1864. Soon afterwards, John Muir began to argue passionately for this protection to be extended to the vast wilderness of mountains and meadows surrounding these two wonderful places. America must not let loggers, graziers and land speculators destroy what could never be restored. Wild places gave people succour and solace; they were essential to the human spirit. Muir said, 'Climb the mountains and get their good tidings. Nature's peace will flow into you as sunshine flows into trees. The winds will blow their own freshness into you, and the storms their energy, while cares will drop off like autumn leaves.' In 1890 Muir and his friends got what they wanted: the federal government declared the entire wilderness a National Park. Muir was named the father of Yosemite NP.

Driving in Yosemite NP poses problems. The park is open day and night all year round, but from about November to the end of May snow closes the roads in the higher parts of the park. Try your very best to come to Yosemite in the summer. Then you can drive to the giant sequoias in Mariposa Grove, reach the high overlooks over the Yosemite Valley at Glacier Point and Wash-

View from the Tioga Road, Yosemite NP

burn Point, and explore the Tioga Road with its extensive views of the Tuolumne Meadows and the Sierra high country. This last drive reaches nearly 10,000 feet as it climbs over the Sierra road summit on the eastern side of the park. John Muir's insistence that the Yosemite wilderness must be saved for posterity is borne out by the splendour of the landscapes along the Tioga Road.

For most people Yosemite Valley is the star attraction. Sculpted by ice and water, its world-renowned physical features are wonderfully bold, dramatic

and photogenic. The valley has sheer sides and a wide, flat floor with huge granite domes and monoliths, hanging valleys, cascading waterfalls, thick woodlands and open meadows. From the Visitor Centre you can walk to the base of the Yosemite Falls, to the Ahwahnee Indian Village, to the must-see Happy Isles, and to Mirror Lake with its handsome views and beautiful reflections of the surrounding landscape. Popular viewing points to see El Capitan, Half Dome, Sentinel Rock, Cathedral Rock and the Bridalveil Fall are at the eastern end of the Wawona Tunnel (California 41) and at the Valley View Turnout just past El Capitan Meadow as you leave the park going westbound on Northside Drive.

Mirror Lake, Yosemite NP

Yosemite Valley from Wawona Tunnel

43

View from Glacier Point: the Yosemite Falls plunge into
Yosemite Valley and the walking trails are clear to see

In summer, spellbinding and wonderfully panoramic views of Yosemite
Valley are seen from Washburn Point and Glacier Point. From the first of
these very high overlooks you can see the Merced River falling over the
Nevada Falls and then the Vernal Falls into the glaciated valley. Half Dome
dominates to the left with the snow-covered high Sierras in the background.
At Glacier Point the Yosemite Falls, the highest waterfall in America, tumble
down from a hanging valley to the Merced Valley where you can pick out the
Visitor Centre building and some of the walking trails leading from it.

View from Washburn Point: the River Merced tumbles into Yosemite Valley while the
Half Dome dominates the left foreground

Yosemite NP to Sequoia and Kings Canyon NPs (155 miles)

Leave Fresno on California 180. It takes two hours to get to Kings Canyon
NP, the road rising 5,000 feet in this time. (For accommodation in Kings
Canyon NP, ring 1-866-522-6966; for Sequoia NP, ring 1-888-252-5757.)
Even more than Yosemite, the roads in these parks are snowbound in winter. The Kings Canyon Scenic Highway is closed all winter, as are most
roads running off the main road known as the General's Highway. Snowfalls may close even this road temporarily. Reports on road conditions in

the two parks can be obtained by ringing 569-565-3341.

Kings River, Kings Canyon NP

Kings Canyon is one of the deepest canyons in America, its rocks gouged out by both ice and water. Sequoia NP is America's second oldest park after Yellowstone. It takes its name from the giant sequoia trees, the world's largest trees by volume, which grow only on the moist west slopes of California's Sierra Nevada between 5,000 and 7,000 feet. Since 1943 the two parks have been managed as one unit. Together they embrace desert foothills, shady forests and the deepest canyons and highest peaks of the entire Sierra Nevada. Like Yosemite NP, their very diverse natural environment boasts hundreds of kinds of trees, plants, flowers, birds and animals. Foraging black bears seek out open and unguarded foods. Ranger advice if a bear approaches is to make loud noises, rattle things and throw pebbles, but always use good judgement and keep a safe distance. Never try to feed them!

California 180 leads directly into Kings Canyon NP through Big Stump Entrance where logging activities once spelled disaster for the giant sequoias. Drive to Grant Grove Visitor Centre and village. The central attraction here is the General Grant Tree – the world's third largest tree. The club-like profile of the sequoias lacks the natural grace of the coastal redwoods, but their mammoth size and physical presence are overwhelming, making even Britain's mighty oaks look puny by comparison. The Visitor Centre tells the story of the logging industry in the second half of the nineteenth century. John Muir said that cutting down the big trees was like selling the rain clouds and the snow and carrying away the rivers.

A walk among sequoias

In the summer California 180 is open as far as the Cedar Grove Visitor Centre. Called the Kings Canyon Scenic Highway, the road explores the glaciated valley of the powerful river and the one-hour drive down is not for the timid and nervous. It descends from over 6,000 feet to 4,500 feet, winding along mountain ledges with steep rock walls on one side and sheer drops to the valley below on the other. The lower you get, the more hemmed in you feel, as huge granite cliffs tower menacingly above you. The river surges as strongly as the Merced in Yosemite NP. A truly impressive piece of road engineering and wonderful views!

Driving south from Grant Grove, the road joins the main road called General's Highway. From here to the Ash Mountain Entrance the road is very winding and very steep in places, climbing as high as 7,600 feet near

Little Baldy. Make sure you stop at the overlooks. For example, 6 miles from Grants Grove at the Kings Canyon Overlook the panoramic view embraces the second largest roadless landscape in the lower 48 states of America. Lodgepole Visitor Centre is the car park for the General Sherman Tree, the world's largest living tree. Some 2,200 years old, this tree is 275 feet high, with branches 7 feet thick and a trunk 103 feet in circumference at the base. Its volume is calculated at 52,500 cubic feet and its trunk alone weighs 1,385 tons. You are in the Giant Forest, explored and named by

The General Sherman Tree, Sequoia NP

Muir himself, and its ecology and history are well presented in the museum there. Four of the five largest trees in the world live in this forest.

Leave Sequoia NP through the Ash Mountain Gate and take California 198 and then California 65 to Bakersfield and Los Angeles. This is a great drive in itself, passing from a luxuriant forest wilderness, crossing through another part of the prolific food basket of the Central Valley, skirting the western extremity of the Mojave Desert, and ending in the great metropolis of America's second biggest city.

3

Burning Deserts

Southern California

This long drive explores two of the Southwest's low-lying deserts – the Colorado and the Mojave. Their scorched, parched and barren landscapes look stark, hostile and forbidding. But there are some nice surprises: a welcome peace and quiet from the madding crowd, unexpected rock features, exotic wildlife and a much richer human history than you would imagine. Those who love deserts say they are refuges for the human spirit and places to reflect on the greater scheme of things.

I-10 catapults you in two hours or so from Los Angeles to Palm Springs on the northwestern fringe of the Colorado Desert. The drive then takes to the Peninsular Mountains for lofty views of the Anza-Borrego Desert SP and then into the desert itself. Driving east, the road passes America's largest saline lake, the Salton Sea, with its impressive Wildlife Refuge for birds. Sand, rock and saltwater are followed by Imperial Valley, a miracle of transformation from desert to bountiful food basket. An old plank road through the huge sand dunes piled high along the border between America and Mexico gives the modern driver a glimpse of what motoring was like in its very early days. Yuma, internationally known for its once infamous Territorial State Prison, has a pedigree history.

From Blythe the road heads west across country used by General Patton to train troops for the Second World War. In Joshua Tree NP, named for the strange trees that are found there, you can see the Colorado Desert slowly give way to the Mojave. The long and lonely road crosses the Mojave National Preserve to Death Valley NP, both areas full of natural phenomena and human activities. Death Valley is recorded as the second hottest place in the world, but it is tolerable in the winter and is the outstanding feature of the entire drive.

Suggested start/finish:	Los Angeles (or Las Vegas)
Length of journey:	About 1,100 miles; 8 to 10 days
Best time of year:	Autumn, winter and spring
Weather:	Annual rainfall no more than a few inches anywhere. From June to September highest daytime temperatures exceed 100°F and lowest temperatures are around 70°F. In December and January highest figures are about 70°F and the lowest about 40°F. Desert temperatures fall at night and in winter they can be sub-zero.

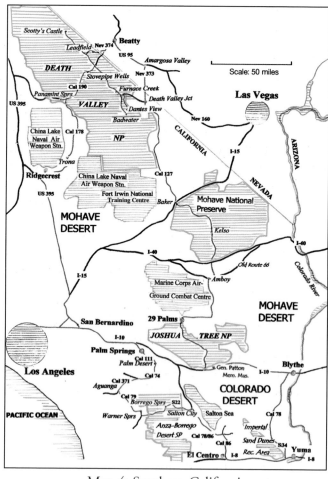

Map 4: Southern California

Drive highlights

Los Angeles to Palm Springs (c. 110 miles)

I went east from Los Angeles on I-10, exiting south on California 111 to Palm Springs. The road cuts down between the steep San Jacinto Mountains to the west and the Little San Bernardino Mountains to the north. Windows need to be shut during this last part of the drive. Wind funnels between the mountains, aided by a massive concentration of whirring wind pumps on the desert floor, create dust storms which sandpaper cars and choke occupants as they pass through the gap.

Palm Springs, once the magnet for Hollywood stars like Bob Hope and Frank Sinatra's 'Rat Pack', has become a fashionable and well-heeled air-conditioned desert resort catering for tourists as well as the super-rich. Remarkably, the largest and wealthiest landowners in Palm Springs are the people of the Agua Caliente Band of Cahuilla Indians. They own more than a fifth of the land there and much of the surrounding countryside. The tribe has lived here for 2,000 years. A visit to Palm Springs Indian Canyons with its magnificent natural scenery is a wonderful experience. From California 111 drive 2 miles to the Indian tollgate, where you can choose from six canyons, park the car and then walk the trails. Try Palm Canyon, which has the world's largest indigenous groves of Washingtonian palms, some 3,000 of them, already full grown before white people first saw them in 1774. Central to the original way of life of the Indians, these trees provided a myriad of products to sustain the tribe, including meal, fruit, tea, baskets, ropes, sandals and thatching for houses. The descent into the canyon is steep and the trail extends for 15 miles. Even a short walk here, however, is well worth the effort. Rattlesnakes are a danger, so be wary. Keep to the paths and leave the reptile well alone if you see one. Visit the Trading Post in this canyon to see examples of tribal art, pottery and baskets and to taste some Indian fry-bread.

Another exciting thing to do is to ride Palm Spring's Aerial Tramway. The cable car whisks you up 8,000 feet of the escarpment face of the San Jacinto Mountain in about 15 minutes. The brown desert dwindles away below as the cable car climbs up the Chino Canyon to the cold, snowy mountain top with its evergreen forests and choice of wilderness trails. There are some spectacular views.

Palm Springs to Yuma (c. 180 miles)

Go south on California 111 South to Palm Desert and then take Highways 74 and 371 towards Temecula before turning south on California 79 at

Palm Springs and the Colorado Desert from San Jacinto Mountains

Aguanda to Warner Springs. Just beyond this small settlement, turn left along the winding S22 to the little town of Borrego Springs, fiercely hot in summer but comfortable in winter. The last stage of this part of the drive is wonderful, the verdant scenery of the mountains suddenly giving way to awesome views of the Colorado Desert with its rocky slopes, desert bajadas, water-eroded badlands and vast flatlands rimmed on three sides by distant mountains.

Millions of years ago, the Colorado River flowed into the Gulf of California through this great depression. The sediments became so deep that the Gulf was forced southwards. Today the Colorado Desert is low-lying, its summer temperatures rivalling those in Death Valley. The Anza-Borrego Desert SP sits in this great depression. The largest of all of California's State Parks, its 600,000 acres of desert keep at bay the rising metropolitan populations and expanding real estates of southern California. You may find this landscape alien, stark and forbidding – nothing like anything you have ever driven through before. It all has a compelling fascination.

The park's entrance is close to the main street of Borrego Springs. The park is so hot in summer that few people go there and the Visitor Centre is open only at the weekends. Built into a hillside, the Centre has an attractive garden with examples of cacti and agaves found in the park. Learning the names and shapes of the main plants and trees helps you to recognise them when you drive through desert landscapes. It is a good test of memory! Half of all the species of plants here are annuals which richly colour the desert between late autumn and early spring if enough rain has fallen for them to grow.

Desert plants of the Anza Borrego Desert SP

A short drive to Borrego Canyon gives another chance to see a palm grove like those in Palm Canyon. This is real wilderness and needs forethought. Take a water bottle and have sturdy shoes, and a hat to protect you from the sun. The round trip takes several hours along a dry and rocky stream bed with cacti, desert willow and creatures such as lizards, quail, rabbits, roadrunners and cactus wrens. In the mating season, between August and December, desert bighorns may be seen. The park is a major refuge for this animal whose yearling is called a 'borrego', the Spanish word giving the State Park part of its name.

In the days before proper roads, crossing this desert was very arduous. In freezing conditions around Christmas time in 1775 Juan Bautista de Anza led a group of friars, soldiers, settlers and children and some thousand head of cattle across this area on his way to settle San Francisco. Four of his campsites and 24 miles of his trail still exist in the park, the landscape still the same as when Anza crossed it. Between 1857 and 1865 the first transcontinental mail services ran through the southern end of the desert. The companies carried passengers as well as mail and they used mules and 'celerity' wagons to cross the desert wastes. These wagons were robust and quick. Time was of the essence, but the ride was very uncomfortable. A steep short walk up the Foot and Walker Pass in Blair Valley leads up the road where passengers walked and sometimes pushed the wagons. It also overlooks the old trail once used by the famous Butterfield Stage Line. Seek the ranger's advice before visiting these places, however!

A copy of the driving tour guide called *Erosion Road* guides you east along S22 to Salton City and the Salton Sea. It points out the natural features of the desert including canyons, playas and arroyos (dry lakes and creeks which temporarily fill with water after rain), and bajadas (raised levels of land at the bottom of slopes formed by piles of rubble sliding down and merging together). Font's Point commands some interest. It gives clear views of the different coloured sediments of the eroded Borrego Badlands.

Salton Sea was created in 1905 when the Colorado River flooded the ancient Salton Sink, a huge depression some 200 miles long and 50 miles wide. It is below sea level, more saline than the Pacific Ocean, and one of the world's biggest inland stretches of saltwater. Providing an excellent habitat for migrating and wintering waterfowl, the southern end of the lake is now a National Wildlife Area, said to be one of the best areas for birdwatching in southern California. Canada geese, snow geese, avocets, stilts, pintails, teals and grebes are common birds in the winter.

El Centro, county seat of the Imperial Valley, is about 40 miles south along California 86 from the Salton Sea. It is the largest city in the USA below sea level. It hardly ever rains and summers are scorching. But in just a few miles from the Salton Sea the change in the landscape is astonishing. The road crosses a great verdant patchwork of livestock enclosures, pastures, orchards, market gardens and cotton fields, all irrigated by water coming from the Colorado River. The construction of the Hoover and Imperial Dams in the 1930s and the opening of the All-American Canal in 1941 have ensured a reliable flow of water from the Colorado River to the Imperial Valley. The mighty river is tamed and harnessed for human benefit, the flooding and destruction of years like 1905 gone for ever. The desert is now an agricultural paradise, one of the richest in the world.

Going east on I-8 from El Centro, the landscape changes abruptly again. On the eastern edge of the Imperial Valley the freeway goes through the Imperial Sand Dunes, the largest mass of wind-blown sand in California. The dune area is 40 miles long and 5 miles wide. Part of it is wilderness, open to walkers and horse-riders but closed to motorists. The dunes visible from either side of the freeway, however, are lined with tyre tracks and alive with joy-riders on motorbikes and buggies who race up and down the dunes in careless abandon. Many of them are 'snowbirds', people escaping the cold north to winter on the dunes in their motorhomes.

Driving the Imperial Sand Dunes 1920s style and modern style

Interestingly, in the early days of motoring, the first road across the shifting dunes was made from wooden planks. Between 1916 and 1926 this road was made from 8-by-12-foot sections, but its serviceability was much in question. Planks wore out quickly, drivers went off the road, and once traffic flow reached 30 cars a day a one-way system had to be introduced. This caused more traffic jams and driver quarrels about who had the right of way. In 1926 the plank road was replaced by a paved road. A monument and interpretive display about the plank road is signposted at the Sand Hills interchange on I-8.

Yuma is another desert resort, not as classy or as renowned as Palm Springs, but worth a two-night stopover. It is Arizona's warmest winter city and boasts that it is the sunniest place in America with 4,133 hours of sunshine a year. Average summer highs exceed 100°F. I was once told by a local that Yumans always walked the shortest line between one piece of shade and the next. He may have been kidding, but it sounded sensible to me. I adopted the practice immediately.

First recorded in the diaries of Spanish conquistadors who arrived here in 1540, the Yuma Crossing became crucial to the history of Arizona and California and to the development of the whole United States. The Crossing is located where two massive outcrops of granite force the Colorado River through a narrow channel some 400 yards wide. It is the best crossing place in the entire Lower Colorado Valley. Anza crossed this spot in the 1770s. Some 60,000 miners used it to cross into California in the first year of the Gold Rush. The Southern Pacific Railroad bridged the Crossing in 1877. Cars first drove across in 1915 when the Ocean-to-Ocean Bridge was opened to link New York and San Francisco. During the Great Depression in the 1930s thousands of people came to California along this route seeking a better life in the far west. In 2000 Yuma became a National Heritage Area, the first place in the west to receive this congressional honour.

The Yuma Crossing SHP commemorates this central theme of the town's history. A lovely picnic spot, its park-like grounds were once the United States Army's main storage and supply depot for all its military posts in Arizona, Nevada, Utah, New Mexico and Texas. The office of the depot quartermaster, the storehouse, the commanding officer's quarters and the unloading dock still exist. A 1907 Southern Pacific locomotive and coach carriage, a 1909 Model T Ford standing on a piece of the original plank road from the Imperial Dunes, and a 1931 Model A truck packed with family belongings for the migration to California during the 1930s are among some of the compelling exhibits of the park.

Yuma's lonely location in the middle of the blazing desert made it an appropriate place to incarcerate killers and robbers, rapists, polygamists and many other bad men and women who roamed about in Arizona Territory in the later nineteenth century. The infamous Yuma Territorial Prison functioned between 1876 and 1909, when it was finally closed because of overcrowding and lack of space for expansion. The main gate, the guard tower and some rock and adobe cells with strap iron doors still stand, giving a good sense of what the prison was like. They have been used as authentic scenes in

Yuma Territorial Prison: guard tower and main gate and old cells built by convicts

many Hollywood Western films. The cells lacked water and sanitation, and they were very hot in the day and cold at night. Bedbugs, cockroaches, black widow spiders and even scorpions added to the discomfort. Daily routines for inmates included working in the stone quarry, prison construction, making adobe and cutting timber. Prisoners who broke the rules were punished by spells in a dungeon or 'dark cell', and those caught trying to escape were clamped with a ball and chain.

Today the prison forms the Yuma Territorial Prison SHP and a visit there is a memorable experience. Surprisingly, a strong case is made that the old prison 'was humanely administered and a model institution for its time'. Paroles and pardons were common, inmates got regular medical attention and access to a good hospital, and many learned to read and write here. Even so, you have to wonder if justice was really served in all cases. In 1889 the outlaw and gunman Frank Leslie, a contemporary of Wyatt Earp, was given a life sentence for killing a prostitute in Tombstone. In prison he spent most of his time nursing prisoners, showing 'exemplary conduct' and proving himself 'a man of good character and education'. He was let out after seven years.

Yuma to Twenty-nine Palms (c. 190 miles)

I booked ahead to get a room in Twenty-nine Palms, a small town on the northern side of Joshua Tree NP. I started early, going west on I-8 to S34, heading north to Blythe and then west again on I-10 towards Indio and Los Angeles.

For more than a hundred miles the landscape is desolate, remote, harsh and inhospitable, unredeemed by any real points of interest. Blythe was the only civilised place for a coffee break. But early in the Second World War the American War Department saw this kind of terrain as an ideal place to train American soldiers in desert warfare. In North Africa Rommel was threatening Egypt and the Suez Canal. Montgomery and the British were badly stretched to stop him. The Desert Training Centre set up by the War Department was huge. It stretched south to Yuma, west across the Salton Sea and almost to Los Angeles, north towards Death Valley and east into southwestern Arizona – 18,000 square miles of land altogether.

The centre's first commander was General George S. Patton. From the outset he set the standards, sharing the harsh and primitive conditions of the desert with his men, demanding high levels of physical fitness (ten-minute miles carrying full backpack and rifle) and rehearsing tactical manoeuvres for tanks and infantry. After four months at the Desert Training Centre Patton was sent to North Africa, but his successors carried on where he left off. Altogether a million soldiers, seven armoured divisions and thirteen infantry divisions were trained in the desert. The General Patton Memorial Museum stands at the Chiriaco Summit on I-10 some 30 miles before Indio. Here you learn more about the man himself as well as life and military activity at the Desert Training Centre. A glance at a map will show that America's armed services still use huge parts of the former Desert Training Centre to prepare for combat in modern warfare.

About 5 miles further west on I-10 is the South Entrance to Joshua Tree NP. The road crosses the Colorado River Aqueduct, carrying water west from Parker Dam into the Los Angeles area. The drive across the park is fascinating and is enhanced by walking some of the short trails and reading the noticeboards along them. This eastern and lower part of the park lies in the Colorado Desert. Creosote bushes dominate the ground. Cottonwood Road leads into Pinto Basin Road, which leads to some fine stands of ocotillo bushes and cholla cactus.

The road climbs over 3,000 feet into the western part of the park, which lies in the Mojave Desert. Turn left into Park Boulevard, following signs for West Entrance Station and the Joshua Tree Visitor Centre. You pass from low desert to high desert. The contrast is quite startling. The landscape now contains impressive stands of Joshua trees, large Mojave yuccas, huge piles of granite boulders that look like the work of giants, and fine viewing points. Joshua trees are the indicator plant of the Mojave Desert. They got their common name from the Mormons, who saw in their outstretched branches a vision of Joshua waving them west to a promised land in the desert. Like the saguaro, the Joshua tree was a tree of life. Indians used it

Joshua Tree

Joshua Tree and granite scenery

to make baskets, sandals and mats; birds make nests in the holes they drill in the trunks; and small animals feed on the fruits and seeds. The best time to see these trees is in spring when the tips of their branches bear large white-green flowers. Squirrels, birds and deer eat the blossoms.

Walks at places like Jumbo Rocks, Queen Valley and Hidden Valley (a cattle rustlers' hideout) encourage photography. So will the tremendous vistas from Keys View, which stands above 5,000 feet. This lofty position overlooks the Little San Bernardino Mountains, the line of the San Andreas Fault, the Coachella Valley and Palm Springs. High in the blue, golden eagles patrol the valleys and desert floors. And at night Joshua Tree NP is a good place to stargaze. The rangers will suggest particular places to go and what to look for. After dark drive back into the park and, for example, look for the Milky Way and some of its constellations.

Twenty-nine Palms to Beatty, Nevada (c. 250 miles)

Without doubt this is a long and lonely drive. I booked ahead and made another early start, going north to Amboy. The road cuts across the low Sheep Hole Mountains and skirts the huge restricted area used as a training centre by the Marine Corps. Bristol Lake is a dry lake in an area once a prehistoric sea. It floods temporarily. Table salt and road salt are dug out here in large quantities. On the other side of the lake Amboy Crater, a 250-feet-high black basalt cinder cone, stands starkly against the browns and yellows of the desert and the vivid blue of the sky. In Amboy itself, part of old Route 66, Roy's Café and Motel is a great place to stop for coffee and take in some 1950s Americana.

Roy's Café and Motel, Historic Route 66, Amboy

The road now goes east towards Needles and then north to Kelso and Baker. Most of this section of road crosses the Mojave National Preserve which is administered by the NPS. More wonderful vistas appear in a vast mountain and desert landscape set aside to preserve America's natural and human heritage. Golden eagles and hawks glide on desert thermals. Quail and mourning doves frequent the canyons and washes. Bighorn sheep, mule deer and coyotes are present but hard to spot. As you would expect, Joshua trees, cacti, yucca and creosote are everywhere. In spring, if the natural conditions are right, the desert boasts vivid displays of wildflowers. Surprisingly, cattle are common on the Preserve, reminders of the once-important ranching industry that thrived here a century ago. To the west side of the road a splendid line of golden-coloured dunes, some 600 feet high, appear along the skyline.

Kelso was once a railway depot and water stop for the steam engines of the Union Pacific Railroad. Built in 1924, it had a train station, ticket and telegraph office, restaurant, reading room and dormitories for railway personnel. Changing technology led to its closure in 1985 and the Union Pacific decided to pull it all down. A public outcry forced a rethink and in 2005 the property reopened, with the station splendidly refurbished and now housing the Information Centre for the Mojave National Preserve. Its privately owned restaurant is another great place for drinks and a meal. Then on to Baker, the road passing a conspicuous line of volcanic cinder cones and black basalt lava flows which have seeped across the desert.

Kelso Depot

The tiny town of Baker marks the end of the Preserve and the start of an 84-mile drive north along California 127 to Death Valley Junction. From here California 190 leads directly into Death Valley NP with accommodation available at either Furnace Creek or Stovepipe Wells. Death Valley Junction itself only had one motel when I drove through there several years ago. In Nevada the truck stop at Beatty has a greater choice of rooms. A two-night stay allows a full day to explore Death Valley.

ACCOMMODATION IN THE DEATH VALLEY AREA
Death Valley NP:	Furnace Creek Ranch and Inn, 303-297-2757
	Stovepipe Wells Village, 303-297-2757
Death Valley Junction:	Amargosa Hotel, 750-852-4441
Beatty:	Burro Inn, 775-553-2225
	El Portal, 775-553-2912
	Exchange Club Motel and Casino, 775-553-2333
	Phoenix Inn, 775-553-2250
	Stagecoach Motel and Casino, 775-553-2419

Death Valley NP

A glance at a map of Death Valley gives an immediate sense of foreboding. Names like Black Mountains, Funeral Peak, Deadman Pass, Badwater, Dante's View and Hell's Gate, as well as Death Valley itself, reflect the mind-set of the people who first crossed it. William Manly, a Forty-Niner who survived Death Valley, wrote that 'the home of the poorest man on earth was preferable to this place'. For years afterwards miners' tales told of satanic beasts and great pockets of poisonous gases killing unwary trespassers.

In the winter of 1849 the remnant of a small wagon train came to a forced halt in Death Valley. The oxen were weak, food was in short supply and the morale of the men, women and children desperately low because they saw no way out of the valley, a route which they had thought was a short cut to California from Salt Lake City. Manly and John Rogers agreed to walk west out of the valley, climb over the mountains and seek fresh supplies for the stricken wagon train. The other people were to wait by a spring for their return, hopefully within 15 days. The two men carried ox flesh and some rice and tea in their backpacks, a rifle and a double-barrelled shotgun. They were gone 26 days, suffering great thirst and hunger, walking west across the Mojave Desert and then back again into Death Valley. They brought supplies and a mule they had obtained at a faraway ranch. Only eight people remained at the spring. The rest had left to make their own ways westwards. Manly and Rogers now walked the Mojave for the third time. They put the women and children on the mule and the oxen, abandoned the wagons and struggled their way to Los Angeles. Manly gave the name 'Death Valley' to the place they left behind.

Death Valley itself is prison-like, enclosed on all sides by walls of mountains. The highest ones, the Panamints, rise over 11,000 feet. Park roads stretch almost the full length and breadth of the Valley – 83 miles from Scotty's Castle to Death Valley Junction; 61 miles from Beatty to Panamint Springs. Driving these roads makes you appreciate the immensity and beauty of the park. Through the windscreen, red sun and blue sky, mountain peaks and canyons, wispy clouds and distant dust storms, heat haze and glare from the salt flats make for wonderful landscapes with ever-changing light and shadows. Beyond the narrow asphalt strips of the park's roads, everywhere is wilderness.

My first-ever journey into Death Valley took me from Beatty through Titus Canyon. A white-knuckle drive of 26 miles, the dirt road strikes off in a westerly direction through the Grapevine Mountains to emerge finally in Death Valley itself, where it joins a main highway in the park. It snakes over

Heat haze, salt and rock in Death Valley

a winding and mountainous trail through Red Pass and the ghost town of Leadfield. No barriers defend you from some precipitous drops along the sides of the track. I drove in a cloud of dust the whole way. Finally, the dirt road plunges down the narrow, twisting gorge of Titus Canyon. Huge masses of bare, twisted rocks hang menacingly above as you gingerly drive the tight bends and steep slopes. Thankful to survive with an undamaged car, I marvelled at the toughness and resilience of the people who lived and worked here nearly a century ago, their only links with the outside world by foot, mule or wagon.

From Furnace Creek it is a 30-mile drive up to Dante's View in the Black Mountains. When I got there, early one April, there was a cold wind and occasional snow flurries. I stood on a narrow ledge and peered down nervously over a sheer drop of thousands of feet to Badwater directly below me. Once upon a time the floor of Death Valley was covered by an ancient lake 100 miles long and 600 feet deep. I saw long lines of naked, dark brown mountains to both east and west, and huge salt flats glistening like virgin snowfields. The road north and south along the valley seemed only a hair's width. Nothing moved! I heard only the wind and the occasional croak of a raven.

I drove down to Badwater, 282 feet below sea level, the lowest point in America. Altogether some 550 square miles of land in the valley are below sea level. The water is saltier than that in the sea. The sun shone out of a clear blue sky and the heat shimmered on the ground. It was shirt-sleeve weather

Death Valley from Dante's View

and time for sunglasses and a hat. I joined the many people walking out on the salt flats, some of whom had strolled half a mile or more from the road. The wilderness had a different face!

Badwater, Death Valley

There are two oases in Death Valley where tourists can find overnight accommodation – Stovepipe Wells and Furnace Creek. Stovepipe Wells has welcomed tourists since 1926. In those days it was called Bungalette City and boasted tents, cabins, electric lights, good food and scenic tours in Buick sedans. Those seeking more realism went on trail rides led by old-time prospectors. When I stayed there some years ago it had wooden cabins, campgrounds, an open-air swimming pool, a general store, a saloon and a comfortable, moderately priced restaurant with table service. I was told a little later on that the waiter who served me was the last living member of the group known as Bill Haley and the Comets. After the meal I lay on the dunes on a clear night looking at the stars. The ranger talked about the moon and its place in Indian life and legend. It was a wonderful evening.

A bronze marker opposite the general store said that this was the spot where the first emigrants to cross Death Valley had to kill their oxen and break up their wagons to survive. Later they found their way out of the valley through Towne Pass. I wondered if this referred to the Manly group. Other miners in a desperate search for water finally found some underground. They marked the spot with a stovepipe and gave the place its name.

Furnace Creek is named not for the intense heat of the summer, but for a small smelting furnace built here by gold- and silver-miners a century ago. The greenery is striking. Thousands of date palms and tamarisk trees provide

Stovepipe Wells

welcome windbreaks and cool shade in a wilderness known to be the hottest and driest place in North America. Here are the four-star Furnace Creek Inn and the Furnace Creek Ranch, much more expensive than the rooms at Stovepipe Wells. Some of the amenities of modern civilisation are here such as well-furnished and air-conditioned cabins, a spring-fed swimming pool, tennis courts, stables, a golf-pro shop, the lowest 18-hole golf course in the world, a steakhouse café, a general store, a post office and a mining museum.

Furnace Creek, Death Valley NP

Scotty's Castle is perhaps the most popular place in Death Valley. It is associated with a much-larger-than-life character known as 'Death Valley Scotty'. A friend of his built the castle as a health retreat, but Walter E. Scott always said that he owned this attractive ranch with Spanish red tile roofs and cream stucco battlemented walls. When his friend died, Scotty moved in and lived there, receiving paying guests and regaling them with the wonderful events of his life. It was said that the flamboyant Scotty was much influenced by the great 'Buffalo Bill' Cody, with whom he had worked for ten years. Scotty became the Valley's biggest tourist attraction – a teller of very tall tales and a con man extraordinaire. The castle is now owned and operated by the NPS.

Another interesting place in Death Valley is the old Harmony Borax works close to Furnace Creek. Borax, 'the white gold of the desert', has been the most profitable mineral in Death Valley's mining history. Harmony operated between 1883 and 1888. Chinese workers living in tents and rough shelters dug the ore out of the ground. It was processed at the site, loaded into huge wagons and hauled by mule teams of 20 animals to the railhead at Mojave 165 miles to the south. The 20-mule team remains the symbol of the borax industry in America. Nowadays the 30-ton loads would need an 18-wheel truck to move this weight. Work stopped in the great heat of the summer, not because it was too hot to work, but because water used in the borax-making process could not be made cool enough for the ore to crystallise.

Harmony Borax Works, Death Valley NP

Two experiences in Death Valley I shall never forget. I was on a dirt track when I suddenly saw a coyote walking towards me in the roadway, its eyes fixed on the car. Rather than get too close to it, I stopped. Amazingly, the adaptable coyotes have learned to live off almost anything, possibly including me. They certainly associate cars with food. This one was wondering if it could get a free lunch from me. I closed all the windows. The animal waited a few minutes, and then walked past just a few yards from the car, heading off into the desert. Another time I came across a tortoise walking in the road. Park literature said it was illegal to pick one up because the reptile might urinate and then die if it did not find water quickly. But it was in danger of

70

being run over. I moved it off the road, keeping it level, and placed it in the shade. Hopefully it stayed alive.

Beatty to Ridgecrest and Los Angeles (c. 230 miles)

I drove southwest across Death Valley, stopping at a pleasant, shady coffee shop in the tiny Panamint Springs and then heading south along Panamint Valley on California 178 to Trona and Ridgecrest. This is hard country. The valley shimmers in the dry heat. Creosote bushes hijack the terrain. Mountains line the sides of the valley and look like sleeping dinosaurs. This was the route of the 20-mule teams and ore wagons. Their journey took ten days to the railhead and wagons often had to be pulled up hills one at a time. The dust, heat, terrain and length of the journey forced the teams to haul water as well as ore – a truly American venture to overcome a hostile wilderness! Today we simply switch on the air-conditioning and enjoy the drive.

California 178, Panamint Valley, Mojave Desert

There are silver- and gold-mining ghost towns in the Panamint Mountains to the east. Information boards on the side of the road tell something of their stories. The town of Panamint boomed for four years between 1872 and 1876 while it worked a silver-rich vein in Surprise Valley. It was a lawless place, and even the prestigious Wells Fargo refused to service it. The mine owners carried the mineral out in cubes each weighing 400 pounds so as to deter thieves. Heavy flooding in 1876 washed away cabins, stores and saloons and wiped out the town. Ballarat, lower down the mountainside, existed between 1897 and 1917. It appears to have been less of a hell-hole than Panamint. Wells Fargo did come here, and there was a jail, mortuary and post office as well as hotels and saloons. Seldom-Seen-Slim seems an interesting character but who he was and why he was so named I never found out.

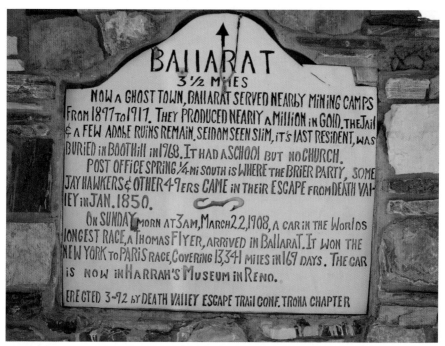

Memories of Ballarat, ghost town

Ridgecrest is a good lunch stop. It has several motels. Go south on California 395 to the junction with I-15 and then south on the freeway to Crestline and various routes into the metropolitan area of Los Angeles. Ridgecrest to Crestline is another hundred miles of the Mojave Desert, quite a tough drive through open desert with very little habitation on the way. There are no roads in the whole of Europe to compare with those of the Mojave.

4

Lonely Places

California, Nevada and Utah

This is the longest of the drives featured in the book. It crosses the Sierra Nevada and the Great Basin twice on this return journey between Sacramento and Salt Lake City. High, rugged, snow-covered mountains and a huge natural basin of sand, salt and sagebrush desert were once formidable barriers to migrants coming overland to the American Southwest. Today, even with modern road surfaces, the vast distances, remote towns, scant roadside services, heavy snowfalls and summer heat can make the journey difficult. The Sierra Nevada and the Great Basin remain lonely places. If the drive gets hard, think of the experiences of the Mormons who settled in the salt desert; the miners and the pioneer settlers and their families who walked much of the way to California; or the young men who rode the Pony Express.

The first part of US 50 roughly traces the tracks of the fabled Pony Express riders who galloped between Sacramento and Salt Lake City (and then on to St Joseph in Missouri). The landscapes remain much the same today – with mountains and desert, and 'Old Sac' and Virginia City. In 1986 a writer in Life magazine declared that the section of US 50 across Nevada was 'the loneliest road in America', a reputation that sticks. Salt Lake City, the first of the Mormon towns in the Southwest, was built where it is because nobody else wanted to stop in the desert, preferring to brave the Great Basin and the Sierra Nevada to get to the rich lands and natural resources of California.

The drive leads round the northern side of Great Salt Lake to lonely Promontory Point, the meeting place of the Central Pacific and the Union Pacific Railroads and one of the great historic places in America. It continues into the Great Salt Lake Desert to follow the tracks of the Bartleson-Bidwell wagon train, the first and the last one to go to the far west using this part of the California Wagon Trail.

The drive returns west along I-80 which traces the routes of the California Trail and the Central Pacific Railroad. The railway and the motorway make the journey across the Great Basin less lonely than the route followed by US 50, but Nevada remains the land of vast open spaces, the land of the miner and the cowboy.

Suggested start/finish:	Sacramento
Length of journey:	About 1,600 miles; 10 to 12 days
Best time of year:	May to October
Weather:	Dry and hot in summer with average maximum temperatures of 90°F or more in the desert valleys of the Great Basin.
	Winters are hard, especially in the Sierra Nevada and the mountains of Nevada and Utah. US 50 and I-80 are year-round roads, but heavy snows close them temporarily or compel the use of wheel chains. A winter drive is possible if weather forecasts are favourable.

Drive highlights

Old Sacramento SHP

'Old Sac' is brimful of restored historic buildings and nostalgia for California in its early years of American statehood. Sacramento was the western terminal of the Pony Express, the Wells Fargo Overland Stage and the Central Pacific Railroad, which all linked California to the eastern states. Sutter's Fort was one finishing point for the settlers arriving along the Californian Trail. Brannan's Store, owned by Sam Brannan, a Mormon elder and California's first millionaire, was one of several hardware and grocery businesses owned by astute shopkeepers who made their fortunes here supplying food, picks and shovels and everything else the miners needed. The very impressive California State Railroad Museum shows the manner of the great human achievements in building the Central Pacific Railroad across the Sierra Nevada in the 1860s.

The bronze statue of the Pony Express rider opposite the former offices of the Wells Fargo Company in 'Old Sac' is a wonderful example of Western art and sculpture with its close attention to every detail of horse and man. It stands at the very place where William (Sam) Hamilton stepped into the saddle to begin the first delivery of Pony Express mail to the east in 1860. Today US 50 follows the early part of the route over the Sierra Nevada and across the Great Basin. Hamilton rode as far as Sportsman's Hall, now a restaurant,

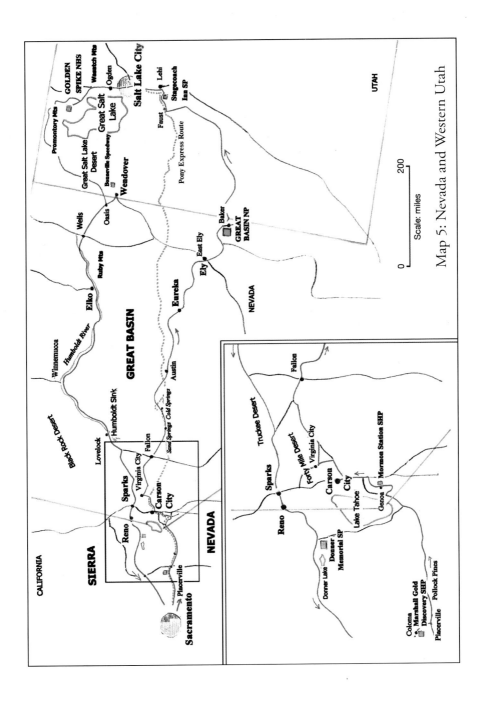

Map 5: Nevada and Western Utah

and handed the mail to the next rider, Warren Hudson, who rode across the storm-swept Sierra Nevada to Carson City before he handed his letters to the third rider, and so on all the way to St Joseph in Missouri, 2,000 miles away.

Statue of Pony Express rider, Old Sacramento

A Pony Express rider was chosen for his youth, fitness, courage and devotion to duty. A California newspaper advert read: 'Wanted. Young, skinny, wiry fellows. Not over 18. Must be expert riders. Willing to risk daily death. Orphans preferred. Wages $25 per week.' Each rider carried 20 pounds of express mail in four pouches stitched to a leather saddlebag which slipped over the saddle and was passed to the next mount in less than two minutes. He rode 10 to 15 miles at full gallop between the relay stations, changing horses at each one, and going 75 miles before resting and then returning to his starting point. A Colt pistol and a Bowie knife were carried for protection and a Bible for spiritual guidance. Riding specially selected horses fed on grain, the rider was more than a match for the grass-grazing ponies of hostile Indians. In his day, the Pony Express rider was an icon of the West.

Sacramento to Carson City (c. 135 miles)

US 50 East from Sacramento, mainly freeway, climbs the slopes of the Sierra Nevada. Make two stops. At Placerville, take California 49 North to the Marshall Gold Discovery SHP at Coloma – another one of the great historic places in America. Here, in 1848, in the forested solitude of the South Fork of the American River, James Marshall found a few specks of gold in the mill race of John Sutter's timber yards. Word was quick to get out. The ensuing Gold Rush galvanised California, America and the world. The Gold Discovery Museum in Coloma tells the story very well. There are some original town buildings to explore, including one where the Chinese workers lived, and a graveyard with tombstones of the people who first went there. The mill race has been rebuilt and you can pan for gold in the icy waters of the American River. James Marshall's figure stands atop a tall statue, his finger pointing to the very spot where he first found gold. Second, just off the main road at Pollock Pines, a plaque outside the old site of Sportsman's Hall records the changeover of the mail from Hamilton to Hudson. Enjoy a coffee at the Pony Espresso about a mile further up the road before returning to US 50.

The federal highway follows Hudson's route, rising up the South Fork of the American River, crossing the mountains at Echo Summit (7,362 feet) and dropping down to the now affluent and busy settlement of South Lake Tahoe with its lakeside views, hotels, shops and casino. Cradled by the Sierra Nevada and Carson Mountains, the lake's deep blue waters are replenished all year round by rainwater and snow-melt from the high ground. Water, land and sky sparkle in the sunshine. Some say the 65-mile drive around the lake is the most beautiful drive in America.

At the state line just north of South Tahoe Lake, I turned east on Nevada 207, drove over Daggett's Pass (7,334 feet) and crossed the Carson Mountains by way of an old toll road. In the old days it saved 15 miles for wagons hauling freight between Sacramento and Virginia City. The road plunges down for more than 2,000 feet into Nevada and the change from cool mountains and green forests to warm, dry desert could not be more abrupt or startling.

Pause for a while in Genoa, Nevada's first settlement and trading post. Set up in 1849 by Mormons sent there by Brigham Young, it traded with wagon trains of pioneer settlers following the eastern base of the Carson Mountains before crossing the Sierra into central and southern California. A trading post here made good sense. Families on the California Trail needed to recover from the hard desert crossing now behind them and replenish their supplies before tackling the Sierra. The Mormon trading post was also the Pony Express station.

Carson Valley, near Genoa, Nevada: both California wagon trains and the
Pony Express travelled along this valley

Near the restored trading post there is a statue of 'Snowshoe' Thompson, a Norwegian immigrant who from 1856 to 1876 braved snowdrifts and blizzards to deliver winter post twice a month between Genoa and Placerville. Taking three days to cover the 90 miles, using hand-made skis and a long pole for balance, Thompson ate crackers and dried beef, drank melted snow, and carried between 50 and 100 pounds of mail on his back. He always made it! Indeed, the ski service lasted much longer than the Pony Express, which collapsed after 18 months with the introduction of the telegraph service in 1861.

Carson City is a good first overnight stop. The silver-domed State Capitol set in very attractive parkland has a compelling statue of Kit Carson, for whom the town was named. Lionised by John Fremont, explorer and publicist of the west, no one knew better than Carson the lonely places of the mountains and the Great Basin. Considered one of the best mountain-men of the day the inscription on the statue said 'His name is synonymous with the wide open spaces and lore of the West, an image we still cherish as part of our freedom and heritage.'

Statue of Kit Carson, Carson City

Elegant Victorian and early twentieth-century houses of historic importance grace the western side of the town. Mark Twain, a newspaper man in the town, used to visit his brother Orion Clemens at his home in North Division Street. Important scenes in John Wayne's final film, *The Shootist*, were shot in the Krebs-Peterson House in North Mountain Street. The Nevada State Railroad Museum shows off rolling stock used by the Virginia and Truckee Railroad Company during the mining of the Comstock Lode. The old locomotives here have appeared in Hollywood Western films.

Nevada 342 leaves US 50 just a few miles north of Carson City and climbs through a countryside littered with disused mines, abandoned buildings and rusting equipment to Virginia City, the centre of Nevada's gold and silver bonanza in the 1860s and 1870s. The Comstock Lode contained veins of silver up to hundreds of feet wide and perhaps was the biggest single mineral strike in history. For a time Virginia City, 'Queen of the Comstock', was

Historic district, Virginia City

the largest city between Denver and San Francisco. It was swept away by fire in 1875, but rebuilt in brick and today survives as Nevada's best historic area, complete with a miners' union hall, courthouse, opera house, churches, schools, mansions and saloons. Here are literally hundreds of historic buildings. The Ponderosa Mine offers underground tours. The Way It Was Museum has a model of part of the Comstock Lode showing tunnels, mine shafts and the new German-inspired honeycombed frameworks of massive timber beams which guaranteed mine safety below ground. Still throbbing with life, Virginia City retains a frontier-like atmosphere and tourists throng the narrow streets, especially at weekends and holiday times.

Carson to Baker: 'The Loneliest Road in America' (c. 400 miles)

In 1986 an article in *Life* magazine described this stretch of US 50 as 'the loneliest road in America'...'It's totally empty ... There are no points of interest. We don't recommend it ... We warn all motorists not to drive there unless they are confident of their driving skills ...' That was like a red rag to a bull! The Nevada Commission on Tourism felt compelled to issue its Official Highway 50 Survival Guide. It dared people to drive the road, get their Survival Guide stamped at various official locations in Fernley, Fallon, Austin, Eureka and Ely, and then receive a certificate signed by the State of Nevada Commission on Tourism as proof that they had indeed driven US 50 through Nevada. Great idea – except that in March 2005, when I drove the road, I found it hard to get a copy of the Survival Guide or find places open to stamp the card. So readers will have to take my word for it that I actually did drive US 50! Like many others, 'the loneliest road' attracted me. I love wild and desolate places and I just had to go there and drive it for myself.

US 50 is a lonely road, especially in winter! It is bleak and monotonous. A two-lane black asphalt strip stretches into tomorrow, crossing wide basins covered in low, clumpy pale green sagebrush and climbing over half a dozen evenly spaced mountain ranges dotted with unimpressive juniper and Pinyon pines. On the flats the high desert stands some 4,000 feet above sea level, but the road climbs well over 7,000 feet at Austin and Ely. Carson to Fallon is 45 miles; Fallon to Austin is 109; Austin to Eureka another 70; Eureka to Ely 77; Ely to Baker 61 – and services are very few and far between them. During the two long days I drove this road in the winter of 2007, I counted 138 cars and 42 trucks on the open highway. A lone cowboy gave me a wave as he rode with his dog along a fence line, but they were alone in a vast and forbidding landscape. A storm was brewing and blackening clouds were filling the sky. Snowfall, breakdown or accident would have been a problem, leaving me stranded miles from nowhere.

The ruins of several Pony Express relay stations exist along US 50. Sand Springs and Cold Springs are worth a stop. The station at Sand Springs still stands, its rock walls defining two large stables and a smaller room for the

81

US 50: 'the loneliest road in America'

Lone cowboy checking fences, Nevada

station keeper and the riders. According to 'Pony' Bob Haslam, a famous rider, his relief rider refused to ride during May 1860 when the Paiutes were on the warpath. Haslam rode his stint for him. On the way back he found the station keeper dead at Cold Springs and no fresh horse available. At Sand Springs he made the keeper leave the station and ride back with him to Lake Tahoe. The next day Sand Springs itself was raided. In all, Haslam rode 380 miles in 36 hours with an 8-hour rest while he waited for the rider coming west to give him the mail. An epic ride! Modern historians, however, cast doubts on such stories. Like 'Buffalo Bill', they say 'Pony' Bob was a braggart who liked to embroider the facts about his adventures along the trail. We will never really know the truth.

US 50 reaches Austin through the middle of a large graveyard full of people from many countries. Austin's boom years were in the 1860s. Look down on Austin today, and you can see how much of its grid-iron road pattern is devoid of buildings. It struggles along as a tourist centre and its farmers grow alfalfa which they truck out to farmers further west. Interestingly, the buildings of the town nearly all lie north of Main Street because this area gets all the winter sunshine – sensible for a town over 6,000 feet high. I talked to a man here called Frank, who was a sailor. Astonishingly, he lived in Austin because he loved the clean fresh air, the winter sunshine, the friendly people and the wide open spaces. He worked out of San Francisco, shopped in Fallon and avoided places like Las Vegas and Reno. He drove me to a high place overlooking the town where I had a bird's eye view of Austin.

Bird's-eye view of Austin, Nevada

Eureka, the 'Pittsburgh of the West', enjoyed a much longer boom than Austin. It was the site of America's first silver-lead smelting industry. Its 16 smelters blackened the sky and rained down soot and dirt everywhere. Welsh and Cornish workers came first, followed by Germans, Italians, Chinese and Jewish people. Like Virginia City, the town was full of saloons, gambling houses, brothels, stores, eating places, theatres and an opera house. Fires almost wiped out the town in the 1870s, but phoenix-like, it rose from the ashes with the handsome brick-built buildings which grace the town today. Unlike Austin, there is no faded glory here. Take a stroll along Main Street South in the vicinity of the finely restored opera house, where shows attract people from Elko, Ely and Tonapah.

Ely remains an important mining community. It benefited from a gold, silver and lead boom in the 1870s, but in the twentieth century the electrical industry and then telecommunications gave the town a much bigger and more permanent boost to its fortunes. Its huge copper reserves still supply the raw material for telephones, light bulbs and computers. Until its closure in 1979, the Liberty Pit at Ruth was the largest open-pit copper mine in the world. Its 80-year working life produced $1 billion worth of copper ore. It is now closed to the public, but you can gaze into it from the Ward Mountain BLM Recreation Area on US 6 South to Tonopah. A ravaged man-made landscape of colossal size in the midst of the grandeur of the Egan Mountains, the pit is a remarkable symbol of the energy and power of private American enterprise in its conquest of the Southwest in modern times. Abandoned mining enterprises often create some compelling landscapes.

Disused mine shaft, Eureka, Nevada

Railway enthusiasts will love the East Ely Railroad Depot Museum. It is the most complete railway museum in the country, with 32 miles of track, station and office buildings still with their original wood furnishings, typewriters, payrolls and other business documents, a large machine shop complex still in use, and locomotives and rolling stock all once part of the Nevada Northern Railroad Company. All of this was donated to the museum by the Kennecott Copper Company after it closed the railway in 1983. The White

Pine Historical Foundation operates local daily excursions of historic steam trains in the summer months but there are ideas to restore a permanent railroad here.

The best scenic spectacle on the 'loneliest road' is Great Basin NP near the tiny settlement of Baker. The park was opened in 1986, just as the article in *Life* magazine was published. It embraces most of the South Snake Range and protects the wonderful variety of habitats and wildlife found there – underground caves and limestone formations; alluvial valleys and sagebrush high desert; forested mountain flanks with pines, Engelmann spruce, Douglas fir and bristlecone; and exposed summits with the remnants of a small glacier and tiny glacial lakes. It can snow here even in July. In 2010 I drove from Baker into the park, following its main road up to 10,000 feet at Wheeler Peak Overlook. The mountain itself reaches up another 3,000 feet. My plan was to walk a trail from the Overlook to the Bristlecone Forest, which has ancient pine trees 2,000–3,000 years old. I failed. Snow covered the slopes and I could not find the way there. It was a great disappointment to me. On reflection, however, it was foolhardy of me to try this alone in winter and I made the right decision to turn back.

Wheeler Peak, Great Basin NP

Underground spectacle: Lehman Caves, Great Basin NP

I had one consolation. I joined a ranger-led party to walk through the limestone and marble Lehman Caves resplendent with stalagmites, stalactites, columns, shields and draperies, all formed by water seeping down through the limestone over many millennia. This was a wonderful experience. Then, near the park exit, I saw a car which appeared to have been driven by a horse. It's amazing what you can see on the loneliest road in America!

A car once driven by a horse, US 50 near the entrance to Great Basin NP

Baker to Salt Lake City (c. 250 miles)

US 6/50 extends into Utah, still riding the roller-coaster of splendid 'basin and range' country and crossing the Sevier Desert to Delta. Mark Twain bemoaned his lot during his stagecoach ride across the Sevier. In *Roughing It*, he deplored the barren silence and solitude, the fierce unrelenting sun and the 'alkali' which coated the animals, driver, coach and passengers in a colourless dust which lodged everywhere, including eyebrows and moustaches. The *Omaha Herald* gave its own advice to stagecoach travellers: 'In winter do not drink liquor, and avoid tight-fitting gloves and shoes or boots; do not smoke or swear inside the coach, do not call attention to places where murders have taken place, and refrain from talk on politics and religion; always spit to leeward and hang on if the horses bolt.' Thank goodness for roads, car radio and air-conditioning!

Keep on US 6 beyond Delta as far as Silver City and then take Utah 36 to Faust. At this point the Pony Express riders were well away from the line of US 50. Their trail across the desert of western Utah and eastern Nevada remains clearly marked by a sand-and-gravel track called the Pony Express Trail National Back Country Byway. The BLM has an interpretive site at Faust where a change of riders took place and mail coach drivers rested their horses. Do not go west beyond Faust Station. The Byway is 100 miles of unreliable road surface and there are no services. Instead drive east on Utah 73 to Stage Coach Inn SP. The inn was an overnight stop for passengers on the Overland Stage Company. Mark Twain once stayed here, and the two-storey adobe and frame building is now restored with original furnishings. Go ahead to I-15 and then north to Salt Lake City.

Salt Lake City and Temple Square

The Great Salt Lake Desert must have been like the Sevier when Brigham Young first saw it in 1847. American wagon trains heading to California mostly gave it a wide berth. But this greatly suited the Mormon leader. He had been told by God that 'this is the place' to build the Mormon paradise on earth. What the Mormons achieved here in the next few decades was a miracle and a unique part of the history of the American Southwest.

Within days of his arrival Brigham Young was planning in detail the construction of Salt Lake City. It was to be 2 square miles of land with 135 blocks of 10 acres each, a town with broad streets and wide pavements, and Temple Square at its very heart. This Mormon Zion was the first planned city of the American Southwest. Young set people to work ploughing and irrigating the land and building a fort. By 1853 Salt Lake City was making clothes, pots and cutlery and it had its own church-operated bank, tithing office and general store. Wagon trains to California called there to buy supplies for their journey ahead. In that year the Mormons broke ground for the temple. Nearly 10,000 men were involved in the laying of its foundations, which included the haulage of 5-ton granite blocks by ox-carts from the Wasatch Mountains. The building of the tabernacle began as soon as the temple foundations were laid. It was all a hugely collaborative and co-operative enterprise resourced by the payment of church tithes in money or in kind by the Mormons and the free labour they gave every tenth working day in lieu of their church dues.

Mormon family and handcart in bronze, Salt Lake City

By the mid-1850s thousands of newly recruited Mormons from England, Germany and Scandinavia were arriving by wagon trains and were directed north and south of Salt Lake City to build towns in its image like Ogden and Provo. Brigham Young even encouraged his followers to walk to Salt Lake, their possessions loaded on handcarts, parents pulling and children pushing. He said that the hardships of the trail strengthened religious faith and spiritual well-being. By 1865 the Mormons had dug 277 canals stretching 1,047 miles and irrigated over 150,000 acres in the desert. Mormon settlements sprang up all over the Southwest as Brigham Young sought to create his huge self-sufficient state of Deseret which was to be almost the size of the entire Southwest Such an idea was doomed to failure. The Americans also believed that God was on their side, that it was their 'manifest destiny' to conquer the whole continent, and no one was going to stop them. They had no time for church-dominated politics or polygamous marriages either. Polygamy was as sinful as slavery!

Today, Temple Square is Utah's number one tourist attraction. The most important Mormon buildings in America are here. Bounded by a wall 15 feet high, the square has shaded walks under great elms and immaculate gardens with lush green lawns, gorgeous flower beds, limpid pools and gushing fountains. There is not one piece of litter or one mark of graffiti. All is a haven of peace and quiet, free from the noise and commotion of the world outside. The great centrepiece is the august granite Gothic Temple with its six spires, adorned with the golden figure of the angel Moroni who is said to have given the Book of Mormon to Joseph Smith. Baptisms, marriages and other sacred services are held here, but the Temple is not open to the public. The huge tabernacle, built for large social gatherings, houses the world-famous Mormon Tabernacle Choir which has sung here since 1867. The Beehive House was built in 1854 and was Brigham Young's home and official residence until 1877. The wooden beehive on top of the house represents hard work and industry, key attributes of the Mormon pioneers. Next door is Lion House (1856), where Brigham Young accommodated some of his many wives.

The immaculate Temple Square, Salt Lake City

Some great panoramic views of the city, the Wasatch Mountains and Great Salt Lake can be seen from the twenty-sixth floor of the Church Office Building. An excellent lunch is served in the Garden Restaurant on the tenth floor of the Joseph Smith Memorial Building. And when the Tabernacle Choir is rehearsing, you can have a free seat. Without doubt a visit to Temple Square is a great day out!

'This is the Place' Heritage Park and Old Deseret Village

This is the other significant site to see while in Salt Lake City. The park and village stand on the very spot where Brigham Young and the first Mormon pioneers emerged from Emigrant Canyon in the Wasatch Mountains in 1847. From this high ground the Great Salt Lake and the Great Salt Lake Desert stretched out before them to the west. 'This is the Place' Monument was sculpted by Brigham Young's grandson to celebrate the first centennial of the Mormons' arrival here. It is a monument not only to the Mormons themselves but to all the people who were involved with them in their trek westwards.

Mormon monument, 'This is the Place', Salt Lake City

Old Deseret Village is a reconstruction of life in Mormon settlements in Utah during the second half of the nineteenth century – log cabins, houses, farms, shops, banks, schools, cemeteries, streets and fences. Everything here is immaculate and reflective of the deep religious faith and zeal of the Mormons, their great pioneering skills, and their strong sense of place in American history and the westward movement of the nation's peoples.

Salt Lake City to Oasis and I-80 (c. 255 miles)

This is another lonely drive. The roads pass around the northern end of Great Salt Lake and cross a long section of Great Salt Lake Desert. They cross the dried-up basin of a huge glacial lake that many thousands of years ago stretched into Nevada. Definitely start with a full fuel tank and plenty of water and food. The highlight of this part of the drive comes early. Leave I-15 at Brigham City and go west for 32 miles on Utah 13 and Utah 83 to Golden Spike NHS. Over 5,000 feet high, the remote and desolate rocky ground of the Promontory Mountains looks out across Great Salt Lake shimmering in the distance. The place belies its huge historical significance.

Promontory Point

Here, on the sunny but cold and icy morning of 10 May 1869, six years before the agreed completion date, the track of the Central Pacific Railroad, building east from Sacramento, was joined to that of the Union Pacific, building west from Omaha, Nebraska. Many people were present – railway workers and sightseers, and dignitaries who were brought in by special trains laid on by the two companies. Tents and booths served refreshments. A huge American flag fluttered in the light wind. The last sleeper to go down was of specially polished mahogany and the last spike used was of pure gold. (Visitors today can still drive in the last spike, but it is only an iron one!) The moment it was driven in, the telegraph operator on site told the nation that the last rail was laid. Guns fired and church bells rang in every part of America. The nation had its first transcontinental railway, a single-line track stretching 1,776 miles across plains, mountains and deserts. It spelled the end of the frontier, the defeat of the wild Indians, a much more vigorous and unified American economy, and a much greater integration of the American west into national life.

10 May 1869: the first transcontinental railway is complete
(Courtesy of the National Park Service, Golden Spike NHS)

The steep and winding grades of railway track through the Promontory Mountains were replaced in the 1920s when a new line was built directly west from Ogden across Great Salt Lake and Great Salt Lake Desert. Silence and solitude have returned to the Promontory Mountains. Yet the great railway building works remain there and the auto tours and the walk along the Big Fill Trail at Golden Spike NHS are well worth a half day's visit.

I returned to Utah 83, went north to I-84, west on the Interstate for about 20 miles, then south on Utah 30 across Great Salt Lake Desert to Rosette, Montello and I-80. The Bartleson-Bidwell party of 34 people, including Benjamin Kelsey, his young wife Nancy and their one-year-old daughter Ann, passed this way in 1841, the first pioneer settlers to go overland to California. Bidwell's diary spoke of 'extensive arid plains, glimmering with heat and salt'. Oxen died from thirst and hunger, the wagons had to be left in the sand and sagebrush, and the pioneers walked the rest of the way, crossing the Great

Basin and climbing over the Sierra Nevada to California – a walk of 500 miles or more. It was an enormous achievement, especially for Nancy Kelsey and her baby daughter, who became the first mother and child to reach California overland from the eastern states.

I-80

West Wendover is 32 miles east of Oasis along I-80. There are plenty of motels here, but my reason for going the 'wrong way' was to visit the famous Bonneville Salt Flats themselves set within the huge and splendid natural amphitheatre of the Great Salt Lake Desert. The world-renowned speedway is 5 miles northeast of Exit 4. Racing begins in July and the annual World of Speed Weekend is held in September.

Driving west on I-80 is much easier than driving east on US 50. But it is still 'basin and range' country with huge open and empty spaces. The road is faster, there are four motorway service stations and seven good-sized towns. However, three of them – Fernley, Sparks and Reno – come in the last 55 miles of a 400-mile drive.

Travelling west on I-80 evokes thoughts about two of the greatest human events in the westward movement of America – the overland migration of miners and settlers to California and the building of the Central Pacific Railroad. The Interstate follows the historic California Trail across most of the Great Basin and then one of its splinter trails across the Sierra Nevada into northwestern California. These parts of the wagon trail were undoubtedly the hardest part of a migration which began in Missouri. Between 1841 and 1870 some 300,000 people made this trek, most of them successfully, to lay the basis of modern California. I-80 also hugs the tracks of the famous Central Pacific Railroad built eastwards from Sacramento to Promontory Point to link with the Union Pacific and form the first transcontinental railway. Wagon trail and railroad track were side by side and great history was in the making.

West Wendover to Reno (c. 400 miles)

Most of the people who trekked along the California Wagon Trail followed the Snake and Raft Rivers in Idaho, then headed southwest to Humboldt Wells (now called Wells) and the Humboldt River. Astonishingly, the Humboldt cuts a flat pathway westwards through the Great Basin, the only river in Nevada to do so. But this 30-day trudge had its own problems. The narrow river dwindled as it went westwards to end in the Humboldt Sink. Food and water for the animals became harder to find. Dust was everywhere, the wagons fanning out to try to avoid the dust from those ahead. Indians, their own meagre desert resources destroyed by the emigrants, took to nuisance night-time raids to steal horses, cattle and oxen to try to deter more people from coming this way.

Red iron posts mark the California Trail between the Raft River and the Humboldt Sink. They each have a number and a quotation about the area taken from diaries written by people who walked along the Trail in the mid-nineteenth century. There are five of these markers in the vicinity of Wells and I managed to find four of them. Standing next to them, you can still see the tracks of the wagons imprinted on the hillsides and in the valleys. To do this I had the benefit of notes I had made from a book edited by Richard K. Brock, entitled *Emigrant Trails West: A Guide to the California Trail from the Raft River to the Humboldt Sink*.

Historical marker, California Wagon Trail

Wells was a campsite for wagon trains and later a depot for the Central Railroad. The town's rather forlorn and under-resourced Emigrant Trail Centre surprisingly had some interesting things to say about life along the trail. The days were long and hard and children did not escape from daily chores like milking cows, herding the family livestock, gathering fuel, cooking food, washing dishes and doing the laundry. There was a whole debate about the best draft animals to use. Oxen were the strongest, cheap to buy, good tempered, ate natural vegetation, needed little harness, pulled well on heavy ground and were less of a target for Indians than horses or mules. But oxen were slow and they did not like hot weather. In the early years, oxen were the most common animals pulling the wagons, but later on horses were preferred because they were faster and therefore reached water and grass ahead of the wagons pulled by oxen.

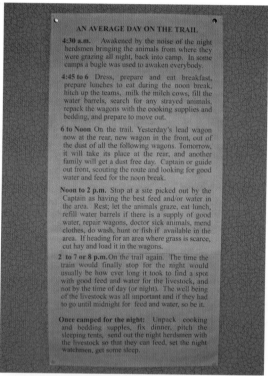

'An Average Day on the Trail', posted in the Emigrant
Trail Centre, Wells, Nevada

Elko began as a railway town by the Central Pacific Railroad, but is now one of the largest settlements in Nevada. Cattle ranches exist all around it and cowboy dress is common. The Cowboy Poetry Gathering in the last week of January and the Cowboy Music Gathering in the final week of June are national events. The town is to be the home of the new California National Historic Trail Interpretive Centre, opening in stages between 2010 and 2012.

The BLM writes that it will be a world-class interpretive facility for the American people, a source of civic pride, an economic engine for the region and a showcase for its work. The Centre will be at exit 292 on I-80, 8 miles west of Elko where the South Fork of the Humboldt meets the main river. This rugged valley was used by several wagon trains in the great migration west. To get here the wagon trains had to climb over the Wasatch Mountains, cross 83 miles of salt flats south of Salt Lake City, and then detour the Ruby Mountains. The Bidwell group actually walked over the Ruby Mountains after crossing Great Salt Lake Desert and this arduous route enhances Nancy Kelsey's achievement. Today, a small diversionary drive from Elko along Nevada 227 to Spring Creek, Lamoille and the Ruby Mountains Scenic Area offers spectacular glaciated scenery, especially along Lamoille Canyon, which is reminiscent of the landscape in Yosemite Valley.

I-80 passes Gravelly Ford, where wagon trains stopped to rest after toiling over Emigrant Pass. From this point wagons used both sides of the river. French Ford was another popular crossing point further downstream. Here wagon trains going to northern California made sure they were on the north side of the Humboldt so that they could leave the main trail at Lassen Meadows near Mill City. When the Central Pacific Railroad was built through French Ford, the place was renamed Winnemucca. This was the name from a local Indian chief who, in return for having the town named after him, promised to stop raiding the wagon trains. The opening of an army fort nearby probably influenced his thinking! For some reason this Indian only wore one moccasin and winnemucca is Paiute for 'one moccasin'. The town was once the hang-out for Butch Cassidy and the Sundance Kid. Cowboy culture is strong in the town, which houses the Buckaroo Hall of Fame and Western Heritage Museum. Winnemucca also celebrates its rich Basque traditions. The Basques came here in the 1870s to mine silver, but stayed to keep sheep. Today, every June, they celebrate their food, costume, dances, parades and feats of strength in the streets of the town, but their numbers are now falling.

The main trail continued along the river to Big Meadows (Lovelock) and the Humboldt Sink. Hay was gathered ready for the next 40 miles of the journey. The main trail now split into two. One went west through the Truckee Desert to the Truckee River and the high Sierra. The other struck southwest across the Forty Mile Desert to Fort Churchill, the Carson River, Carson City, Genoa and Carson Pass. Either way was hard going. However, both Peter Lassen and William Nobles (see Chapter 1) left the main trail before Lovelock, choosing to cross the Black Rock Desert – which proved equally as bad as the Truckee and Forty Mile Deserts. Lassen went to Goose Lake, almost on the Canadian border, before swinging back southwest to his ranch on the Sacramento River, a long and very arduous route which almost caused Lassen to be lynched by the settlers with him. Nobles' route, pioneered later, was a much shorter and more popular trail running almost due west to the Sacramento River at Shasta, not far north from Lassen's ranch near Redding.

Reno to Sacramento (c. 130 miles)

I-80 follows the Truckee Route, climbing up the Sierra Nevada through Donner Pass. Here the well-signposted Donner Memorial SP commemorates the greatest tragedy in the history of the California Trail. It makes for a sobering visit.

The Reed-Donner Party: bronze sculpture at the base of the 'This is the Place' memorial, Salt Lake City

The Donner Party's expedition was a disaster from beginning to end. In 1846 it was the last group to leave Missouri and it started too late in the season. The expedition wasted much time hacking a 36-mile road across the Wasatch Mountains. It lost 100 oxen and wagons and supplies crossing the waterless Great Salt Lake Desert. A row over oxen led to the killing of one of the teamsters by James Reed in the area of Gravelly Ford. He was banished from the wagon train. He and a friend rode on to Sutter's Fort in California, leaving behind his wife and four children. The Donner Party struggled on, harassed by Paiutes, reaching the Truckee River late in October. They were in low spirits and had no food. Heavy rains and snow frustrated three attempts to cross Truckee Pass (now called Donner Pass). The wagons were separated: some at Truckee Lake sheltering in log cabins, the others back at Alder Creek where Donner's wagon had broken an axle and the people with him were reduced to sheltering in flimsy tents and lean-tos. Altogether 91 people were stranded, 41 of them children. In December, 10 men, 5 young women and 2 boys got over the pass, but blizzards and starvation killed most of them, their bodies being roasted and eaten by those still alive. Only 2 men and the 5 women made it through. Between February and April in 1847 four relief parties, including one with James Reed, managed to evacuate the two camps. Survivors confessed to cannibalism. Of the 91 emigrants stranded in the two camps, only 49 survived, including all the members of the Reed and Breen families. George Donner and his wife died in camp.

'Waiting for Rescue': wood carving in Donner Memorial SP, California
(Courtesy of California State Parks, 2011)

'Rescue Team for the Donner Party': a painting in the Donner Memorial SP
(Courtesy of California State Parks, 2011)

The Sierra Nevada was the greatest physical obstacle not only to wagon trains, but also to the building of the Central Pacific Railroad. The railway had to climb 7,000 feet from Sacramento to the mountain summits some 100 miles away and then descend 3,000 feet to the Humboldt Sink and the Great Basin. This first section of the railway, built between 1865 and 1868, was a work of giants – America's greatest single piece of engineering and construction in the nineteenth century.

James Strobridge and his Chinese and Irish construction gangs building the Central Pacific Railroad *(Image courtesy of Lee Witton, archivist, and Ogden Railroad Station, Utah)*

Iron rails, spikes, locomotives and rolling stock from eastern America got to Sacramento around Cape Horn. Schooners carried timber for sleepers and bridges from northern California and Oregon. Thousands of Chinese and Irish workers were hired and ruled with an iron fist by James Harvey Strobridge, the construction boss. The energy, zeal and resolution of the workers – especially the Chinese – were incredible. Working with picks, shovels, wheelbarrows, handcarts, gunpowder and even nitroglycerine, they erected huge trestle bridges and made cuttings, embankments and ledges along steep slopes. In blizzards, avalanches and deep snow they dug and blasted six tunnels to get to the summit at Donner Pass and then nine more to get the railway down to the Nevada Desert. The Summit Tunnel itself was nearly a third of a mile long and 20 feet high and took nine months to complete. Thirty-seven miles of snow-sheds were also built, using 65 million board feet of timber, to protect the tracks from snow and to keep the trains running, a work still in progress even after the transcontinental railway opened.

The first locomotive of the Central Pacific Railroad and the snow-shed above Donner Lake: display in the California State Railroad Museum, Sacramento
(Courtesy of California State Parks, 2011)

Driving I-80 over the Sierra today, you only glimpse these famous old wagon trails and railway tracks. Yet the immensity of the mountain barrier is very palpable and you have to marvel at the tenacity of the pioneer families and the railway builders who struggled so valiantly to overcome it. Places such as Donner Pass, Emigrant Pass, Cisco, Dutch Flat, Bear Valley, Colfax, Auburn and Roseville remain on the map to mark the routes of wagons and trains across the cold, formidable granite mass of the Sierra.

Road and railway routes at Donner Pass

5

High Plateau

Southern Utah

This drive traverses one of America's wildest places, the high and desolate Colorado Plateau in southern Utah. Much of it is along lonely two-lane highways which cut through magnificent sandstone and limestone scenery – wilderness landscape at its splendid best, where human history is scant and people puny, insignificant and superfluous against gargantuan rock surroundings. The outstanding highlights of the journey are the five magnificent National Parks, Arches, Canyonlands, Capitol Reef, Bryce Canyon and Zion, and the National Monument called Cedar Breaks – all unforgettable testaments to the awe-inspiring and incredible ways in which physical forces form and shape the land. One of the loneliest roads is Utah 12. Above 10,000 feet high in places and with some great views across the Henry Mountains, this winding, scenic road cuts across the top of the Grand Staircase Escalante NM, passing several State Parks and the small Mormon towns of Boulder and Escalante, whose families are the descendants of the people who settled there some 150 years ago.

Neither Spanish explorers nor American mountain-men penetrated here. This formidable task was achieved by John Wesley Powell, 'the Major', as he was known to his intrepid boatmen. In 1869 and 1871–72 Powell made two perilous journeys from Wyoming down the wild and ferocious rivers of the Green and the Colorado to the western end of the Grand Canyon in Arizona. This drive begins at a crossing of the Green River where Powell's men rested in 1871 and a museum there now pays tribute to his great work. The journey includes some other places which featured in Powell's explorations.

Utah is America's Mormon state, but even the Saints, as the Mormons called themselves, found life hard in southern Utah and their settlements are small and few in number. But at the end of the drive, in the extreme southwestern part of the state, you reach the Mormon 'Dixie' where the summers are hot and the winters warm and the towns of Cedar City and Saint George offer the comforts of modern civilisation.

Suggested start/finish:	Las Vegas or Salt Lake City
Length of journey:	About 1,250 miles (including the miles to and from Las Vegas or Salt Lake City); 6 or 7 days.
Best time of year:	Late May to late September but remaining cool, especially at Cedar Breaks NM.
Weather:	Cold and snowy for many months although the Parks are open all year round. Summer temperatures can reach over 90F.

NB: Carry water, food, a mobile phone, warm clothing and strong shoes. Fill your tank before leaving US 191. Fuel is scarce between Blanding and Panguitch

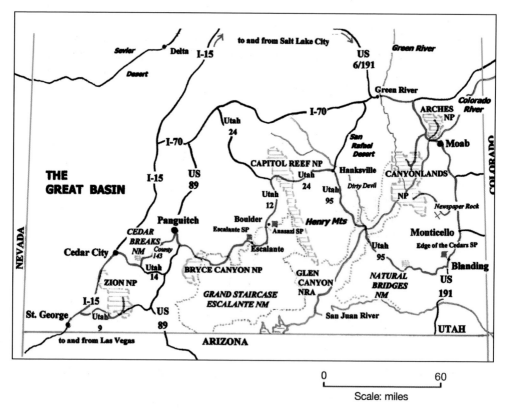

Map 6: The Colorado Plateau

Drive highlights

Green River to Moab (c. 50 miles)

Drive to the small settlement of Green River on I-70 and stop at Green River State Park, its shaded cottonwoods the start for seasonal boat and raft trips along the river. You enter Powell country and the small but interesting John Wesley Powell River Museum is definitely worth a look.

John Wesley Powell has been described as one of the great men of America, a person of iron will, great persistence and a wonderful originality of mind. He took a deep interest in geology, botany, zoology, archaeology and Indian affairs. Known as the 'Conqueror of the Colorado', Powell made his name in 1869 by leading a daring expedition with ten men and four small wooden boats along the Green and the Colorado Rivers, a very hazardous journey of more than 1,000 miles through deep, unknown canyons full of waterfalls and rapids. He began at the Union Pacific Railroad crossing of the Green River in Wyoming and ended on the Colorado River at the western end of the Grand Canyon in Arizona. The achievement was made more remarkable by the fact that Powell had only one arm, the other shot off at the battle of Shiloh during the American Civil War. While afloat, he sat in a chair strapped to the deck of the lead boat, the *Dean*, reading the signs of the water ahead and shouting instructions to guide his boatmen downstream.

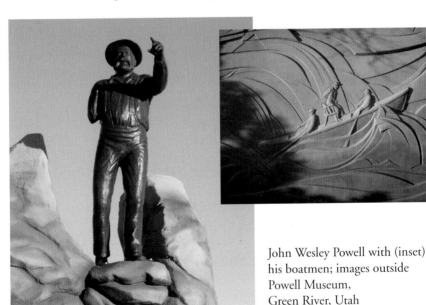

John Wesley Powell with (inset) his boatmen; images outside Powell Museum, Green River, Utah

His standing was enhanced by a repeat voyage in 1871–72 which made detailed studies of the plateaus, mesas, cliffs and canyons of the huge and hitherto mysterious and largely unknown Colorado Plateau. These studies included the first sketches, paintings, photographs, maps, botanical specimens and writings of the area's natural and human history. This work was influential in the creation of the US Geological Survey and the US Bureau of Ethnology, which Powell directed between 1881 and 1895.

Powell's second expedition reached this drive's starting point on the Green River in Utah late in August 1871 after tough, heart-pounding rides down 100 rapids in the 133 miles length of Desolation Canyon and Gray Canyon. The ten men camped on a smooth sandy beach in this open valley – silent, desolate and barren except for a few cottonwoods. (From the road bridge the scene upstream is probably little different from what Powell saw 140 years ago.) The boats were hauled ashore, repaired and caulked with pine gum collected in Desolation Canyon. The men had received fresh supplies of food and water upstream at the mouth of the Uinta River, but these were getting low by this point.

Powell was not with the expedition when it got here. He had gone ahead to the Uinta to check that the next issue of supplies would be delivered on time at the mouth of the Dirty Devil River, south of the confluence of the Green and Colorado. He was told that the fresh provisions would not be there. No one knew how to get to the Dirty Devil overland – not even Jacob Hamblin, the great Mormon explorer, who had been forced back after trying to swim animals and packs through sheer-sided canyons full of rushing water. Powell himself rode hundreds of miles to find provisions, which he brought back by packhorse with the help of another member of the Hamblin family. These supplies proved insufficient, however, and it meant rations and hardship for everybody for the next part of the journey. At this point Powell and his men were still nearly 600 miles away from the western end of the Grand Canyon. Immediately ahead were the Labyrinth and the Stillwater Canyons, and then they would join the Colorado River and face the formidable Cataract Canyon.

The red rock town of Moab is an hour's drive away from the Green River, the road dropping steeply through Moab Canyon. Between 1830 and 1850, Moab was a stopping place on the Old Spanish Trail, a trade route between Santa Fe and San Gabriel Mission in southern California. Mexican pack trains carried silver, woollen goods and blankets west, and horses and mules were driven back east, many stolen from ranches in California. Mormon missionaries arrived in Moab in 1855 and gave it its biblical name. Outlaw gangs like Butch Cassidy's Wild Bunch later frequented the town and horse thieves hid cattle round about. The splendid sandstone scenery here has provided locations for many Hollywood Westerns, including the film *How the West was Won*. The old Mormon church is now the Hollywood Stuntmen's Hall of Fame.

Moab overlooks the Colorado River. Today it is a tourist centre with a good number of motels and shops. Temperatures are warm in winter. There is much to do, including boat trips, rafting, cycling, walking, jeep tours and scenic flights. It is the base for driving the splendid Arches NP, Dead Horse Point SP and the 'Island in the Sky' section of Canyonlands NP. I stayed for two nights to make these visits. Neither Arches nor Canyonlands have park accommodation (for hotel details ring the Moab Information Centre, 435-259-8825 or 800-635-6622).

The entrance and Visitor Centre to Arches NP is 5 miles north of Moab on US 191. It takes four to five hours to drive the nearly 30 miles of paved roads within the park, allowing ten minutes at each viewpoint. Rugged, stark and austere, this is high desert country of sand and sandstone, monolithic rock structures and scant vegetation. The red landscape glows against the snowy peaks of the La Sal Mountains and the wonderful clear blue skies. Daytime summer temperatures can reach 110°F. Venturing from the car to explore the walking trails of this beautiful but harsh environment means hat, sun cream, sturdy shoes, plenty of water (1 gallon per person for a day) and food.

The park has over 2,000 arches with openings of at least 3 feet, the best collection of stone arches and unusual rock formations in the world. Some arches are imaginatively named – Delicate Arch, Fiery Furnace, Three Gossips, Devil's Garden and Parade of Elephants. There is much wildlife here as well. Look for the desert bighorn near the park entrance, mule deer in the Devil's Garden area, desert cottontails and jackrabbits at dawn and dusk, and the solitary coyote forever foraging for his supper. I did not see a bright green western collared lizard with its distinctive black collar, but the Visitor Guide Book said it is the park's most photogenic lizard and very cooperative with photographers.

Dead Horse Point SP is an island mesa 2,000 feet above the Colorado River. A natural corral, wild horses were once driven there by cowboys who sorted out the best animals and left the rest to find their way off the mesa. Unfortunately they failed to do so, but they gave the area its name. The overlook just beyond the Visitor Centre gives you magnificent views of the Colorado River and Canyonlands NP.

Four images of the sandstone scenery in Arches NP

Canyonlands NP is Utah's largest park, over four times bigger than Arches. In summer the land is hot and dry, in winter cold and snowy. The Green and the Colorado meet here, the main river becoming much deeper and faster as it travels through Cataract Canyon, whose walls stand as high as 2,000 feet above the racing, plunging water. One of Powell's boatmen referred to this place as 'the grim jaws of the Colorado'. It remains a severe test for modern rafters.

The park is a huge surviving fragment of America's Wild West. Powell put it very simply. He said, 'The landscape everywhere, away from the river, is rock.' The rock takes many forms – mesas, rims, cliffs, canyons, towers, arches, pinnacles and spires – all awe-inspiring and mammoth in scale. Humans are tiny specks in the majesty of the natural world.

Canyonlands NP

'Island in the Sky' is the highest part of Canyonlands and stands as a broad tableland some 6,000 feet high inside the great V-shape formed by the confluence of the Green and the Colorado Rivers. Below the mesa, over 1,000 feet down, spreads a wide, flat sandstone platform known as the White Rim, itself 1,000 feet above the two rivers – three quite separate worlds! In the 12 miles from the Visitor Centre to Grand View there are a number of stunning vistas: Shafer Canyon, Mesa Arch, Green River Overlook, Buck Canyon Overlook, Orange Cliffs Overlook and the great climax of Grand View Point itself, from where you can see for 100 miles across the Colorado Plateau. Ravens with their four-foot wingspans and wedge-shaped tails love to float in the air currents wafting around the rims of the mesas.

'Island in the Sky', Canyonlands NP

Grand View, Canyonlands NP

Moab to Blanding (c. 75 miles)

The drive to and from the Needles is quite a long one and it is wise to pre-book a room either at Monticello or Blanding, two small towns settled by Mormons in the 1880s. On Utah 211 is Newspaper Rock Recreation Site, a rock wall with carvings made over a span of a thousand years of Indian history. The images are unintelligible to the white tourist but an historic and spiritual journey for the modern Hopi and Zuni Indians who are directly descended from the prehistoric Anasazi people. Massive red- and white-striped sandstone pinnacles dominate the Needles area and give it its name.

Newspaper Rock, Monticello, Utah

The Needles, Canyonlands NP

In Blanding children will enjoy the Dinosaur Museum and adults a browse in the town's few trading posts which deal in Indian arts and craft. Edge of the Cedars SP is also well worth a look. It preserves the remains of an Anasazi village, including houses and a large kiva where religious ceremonies were held, and an excellent collection of prehistoric pottery. Anasazi culture reached its highest expression in this area. Cortez and the wonderful Mesa Verde NP are 60 miles away from Monticello on US 491. If you enjoy Indian prehistory and have several days to spare, then drive into Colorado to see much more spectacular forms of Anasazi building and architecture, all accomplished well before Columbus arrived in the New World. Note, however, that this area is part of a much longer drive in 'Indian Country' described in Chapter 7.

Blanding to Panguitch (c. 305 miles)

This is 300 miles of very lonely road. Except near the National Parks themselves, there is very little traffic. The two-lane highways are thin strips of civilisation through hostile wilderness. Utah 95 and Utah 24 cross the heart of the San Rafael Desert. Utah 12 rides through forests and plateaus as high as 10,000 feet. Apart from the two parks, the small settlements are few and far between and services are very limited. I do not remember any between Blanding and Hanksville, a distance of nearly 130 miles. Generally this is no place to break down or feel unwell! If you do stop, never go far from the car. Your car is a place of shade and refuge as well as a means of transport. Waiting for another vehicle to come by and stop to give help may take a long time.

From Blanding take Utah 95 West to Hanksville. The road skirts the southern end of the huge Manti-La Sal National Forest where land rises above 9,000 feet. Thirty-five miles from Blanding, take Utah 275 to Natural Bridges NM. This small diversion and loop road offers striking examples of the making and the destruction of natural bridges in sandstone country. The biggest bridge, Sipapu, stands in its prime, towering 220 feet above the canyon. Graceful and symmetrical, its buttresses stand away from the present river and escape heavy erosion. Kachina Bridge, almost as high as Sipapu, is huge and bulky, its archway still being formed by the stream. The third bridge, Owachomo, is under attack from frost, rain and blowing sand. The remains of buttresses still visible on the canyon wall betray the former presence of a fourth bridge now overcome by erosion.

Utah 95 continues north across red rock wilderness to bridge the Colorado River south of Cataract Canyon. Here is another place where Powell's two expeditions camped. Cataract Canyon was upstream. A member of Powell's second expedition wrote that its treacherous waters gave the boatmen all the work they could desire.

It was about here that the 1869 expedition first sighted the 'Unknown Mountains'. Powell later named them the Henry Mountains – the last range of mountains to be discovered in America. Seen to the west side of the road, the highest peak reaches 11,371 feet. And it was here that the men of the first expedition found the water of the tributary joining the Colorado to be muddy and undrinkable. They called it the 'Dirty Devil'. For the second expedition arriving here, there were no fresh supplies of any kind. The next supply point was 100 miles downstream and the second expedition was forced to survive on the barest of rations. (In Powell's day the Dirty Devil flowed into the mighty Colorado, but today his campsites and the confluence of the two rivers are lost under the waters backed up here by the building of the Glen Canyon Dam in the 1960s. They are now an unidentifiable part of the Glen Canyon and its National Recreation Area.)

In March 2005 I stopped at Hanksville, a small, dusty, forlorn settlement in the middle of nowhere. Fuel, food and beds were limited, although a brand new motel was about to open. The motel keeper was eccentric, with a dinosaur sense of history which seemed to stop in 1776. When he learned that I was British, he said America was much better off since it rebelled against George III and he asked me how I could still endure living in England under such tyranny. But he was kindly, ringing across the road to ask the store to stay open while I went to buy a hamburger and some food for the next day.

Utah 24 leads west from Hanksville to Caineville and Capitol Reef NP. The desert is barren and inhospitable. Powell mapped this area in 1872. The road follows a river named by Powell for John Charles Fremont, an earlier overland explorer whose expeditions and publications had done much to attract people into the American west, including Brigham Young and the Mormons. Later on, Fremont's name was given by archaeologists to the prehistoric hunters and gatherers who once lived here.

Utah 24 follows the serpentine Fremont through the northern part of Capitol Reef NP. The park embraces and protects a huge fold of land 100 miles long which was thrust up out of the earth 65 million years ago. Since then it has been eroded by wind and water into a confusing barrier or 'reef' of cliffs, domes, monoliths, canyons and basins. The river and rainfall captured in the basins (waterpockets) made the area an oasis for prehistoric people, the Mormons and wildlife. No wonder that this was another favourite hideout of Butch Cassidy and his outlaws. The red, brown, grey, pink, blue and white rocks are so striking here that the Navajo Indians call the area 'the

Visitor Centre, Capitol Reef

land of the sleeping rainbow'.

Many of the natural and cultural features of the park are easily accessible from the main road and the Visitor Centre, an impressive building which blends superbly with the natural landscape. You can drive or walk to the 'Capitol Dome', 'The Castle', 'Chimney Rock' and 'Grand Wash', gaze at Fremont Indian petroglyphs, and visit some surviving Mormon buildings in the once thriving Fruita District where deer now roam freely. The farming abilities and the self-sufficiency of the Mormons in such a wild and remote place have to be admired. The Behunin family lived in a one-roomed cabin near the Fremont River in the 1890s. The older children slept outside, the girls bedded down in a wagon box in the yard and the boys in an alcove in the nearby rocks. A peep inside the old schoolhouse with its handbell, inkpots and single wooden desks and chairs brought back some memories of my own primary school days. The orchards contain 2,600 fruit and nut trees and they continue to produce apples, pears, oranges and apricots under NPS ownership and management.

I went on west towards Torrey and then south on Utah 12, a road heralded as one of America's most scenic byways. It climbs round the eastern side of Boulder Mountain, reaching a high point of 9,400 feet. Just past the

Fruita Schoolhouse

Mormon settlers of Fruita built the school in 1896. Later alterations and repairs have changed it very little.

Eight grades were taught in one room — as many as 26 pupils, and as few as 8. In the early years school was open only during winter months. The rest of the time children helped with the farming and homesteading. More than a classroom, the building was a meetinghouse and Sunday school, and a Saturday night social center. The last class was held in 1941.

Fruita School Class 1911-12

The Mormon school, Capitol Reef NP

summit, look for the Steep Creek and Homestead Overlooks which provide sweeping panoramic views of the Waterpocket Fold and the Henry Mountains and later on glimpses of Powell's Point (10,188 feet), a landmark survey point used in the second expedition. The road then falls to the small town of Boulder, where it follows the northern boundary of the huge Grand Staircase

Escalante NM westwards to Bryce Canyon. Between Boulder and Escalante the scenic road follows a high, narrow ridge called 'Hell's Backbone' – not a place to be in bad weather!

Henry Mountains

Powell's Point

Hell's Backbone

The Grand Staircase is a series of differently coloured cliffs, each named for their distinctive colour – Pink, White, Vermilion and Gray. This was the last place in the continental United States to be mapped. The cliffs step down in huge terraces across southwestern Utah, finally falling into the Grand Canyon in northern Arizona. A land of plateaus, cliffs, canyons, waterfalls, natural bridges and arches, dinosaur fossils and Anasazi ruins, this area is very much a microcosm of the Colorado Plateau itself. It remains a high, rugged and remote frontier. Its side roads lack services and tarmac, and I chose not to explore them.

Boulder had no road before 1935 and until then it relied on packhorses to deliver its daily supplies along 'Hell's Backbone' from Escalante. Boulder's name comes from the huge mountain to its north. Escalante is named for the Spanish Franciscan priest Father Silvestre Velez de Escalante, who explored parts of Utah in 1776. Both towns have historic houses and barns and people still weave, quilt and crochet like their Mormon forebears in the late nineteenth century. Anasazi SP in Boulder marks another important prehistoric Indian site west of the Colorado River. Self-guiding trails wind through numerous house ruins. There is a replica of a six-roomed prehistoric house and a good Visitor Centre with local artefacts. Escalante SP has a self-guiding nature trail, freshwater lakes, a fossilised ancient forest said to be haunted, and dinosaur bones. Both parks have good picnic spots.

Panguitch is a good place to stay the night. About 1,500 people live there and 40% of them are said to have English ancestors. The original English settlers here came in response to Brigham Young's recruitment drive in the mid-nineteenth century. He told them to raise cattle and sheep, and livestock remains an important feature of the town's economy. Some original Mormon homes still dot the town. The Daughters of Pioneer Utah presently occupy the Bishop Store, the tithing building once used by the early Mormons. They are a source of information about the town's history. Another original building is now a restaurant called 'The Cowboys' Smokehouse'. You cannot miss it: outside on the pavement stands a life-size image of John Wayne brandishing his rifle and urging you to go inside. Rooms are cheaper in Panguitch than in Bryce NP. (For reservations in the local area ring Garfield County Travel Council on 1-800-444-6689. To book rooms at Bryce Canyon Lodge, ring 435-834-5322. The Lodge is open from 1 April to 31 October.)

Bryce Canyon NP is a unique and magical place. At 8,000–9,000 feet, the park stands on the eastern rim of one of the highest plateaus in Utah. Standing on the Pink Cliffs, the topmost step of the Grand Staircase, you look right down the massive cliff lines of the Grand Staircase Escalante NM which end finally in northern Arizona some 200 miles away. Around you are forests of pine, spruce and fir, groves of aspen and meadows ablaze with wildflowers from late spring to the end of summer. Snow comes from November to March, but days are warm from May to October. At night, stars and constellations sparkle like jewels in a black velvet sky – a wonderful place for stargazing! The night sky is not polluted by lights from urban areas, the rangers are knowledgeable astronomers, and the telescopes are powerful ones.

Streams of the Paria River have carved the rim of the canyon into amphitheatres and over millions of years water, ice and wind have eroded the sedimentary rocks into a myriad of fantastic shapes, called 'hoodoos'. A Paiute Indian Legend says that before the Indians the Legend People lived there. They were of many kinds – birds, animals, lizards and such things – but they looked like people. For some reason the Legend People in this place were bad. Coyote turned them into rocks. You can see them now, some standing in rows, some sitting down, some holding onto each other. You can see their faces, with paint on them just as they were before they became rocks…

Even modern imaginations run riot, with single rocks earning names like 'Queen Victoria', 'Thor's Hammer', 'Sinking Ship' or 'Alligator', while groups of rocks are said to mimic 'Wall Street', a 'Silent City', or 'Fairyland Canyon'. Interconnecting walking trails lie below the rim and provide some of the best scenery in the park. It is truly spellbinding!

Striking landscapes at Bryce Canyon NP

Bryce Canyon gets its name from Ebenezer and Mary Bryce, the first Mormons to settle in the area. They dug ditches from the Paria to irrigate their land, built a road to the forest to haul timber to build their cabin, supervised the building of a church, and raised their family here.

Panguitch to St George (c. 130 miles)

Utah 143 South leads to Cedar Breaks NM on the Markagunt Plateau, another really spectacular scenic wonder rivalling that of Bryce Canyon itself. The 5-mile Monument Road takes you up well over 10,000 feet to another brilliantly coloured rock amphitheatre and to the forests and meadows of the high country. It is cool even in the height of summer. The attractive Visitor Centre is open from late May to late October. The fresh, thin air makes for harder walking, but the splendid views make it well worth the effort. Four overlooks peer down on a huge amphitheatre some 3 miles wide and 2,000 feet deep. Red, yellow and purple cliffs, spires, arches and columns spread out before you, the view changing with each vantage point. Again, the imagination runs riot, with castles, palaces and cathedrals rising up towards you. From Point Supreme, the 2-mile Ramparts Trail leads round the great bowl of rocks, giving yet another viewpoint of the Cedar Breaks amphitheatre. From the Chessman Ridge Overlook, 10,467 feet high, there is another 2-mile walk along the Alpine Pond Trail which leads you through forests of spruce, fir and quaking aspen and lush meadows of grasses and wildflowers.

High Country above 10,000 feet, Cedar Breaks NM

Ravens, nutcrackers and swallows abound as well as mule deer, squirrels and chipmunks. The secretive and rarely seen mountain lion reigns supreme here.

Beware snowfalls! Several years ago I crossed the Markagunt Plateau in March. I was very lucky to make it. Heavy snow had fallen just previously and snow ploughs had made narrow pathways along the road. These snow canyons had banked-up walls on either side up to 10 feet high and passing another vehicle was not easy.

Zion NP is west on Utah 14 and south on I-15. I interrupted this part of the drive to stay overnight in Cedar City, settled by the Mormons who were sent there to start an iron industry in 1851. There was no shortage of skills. Young sent English, Scottish and Welsh miners to work the plentiful local deposits of iron ore. Iron Mission SP now stands at the place which was the first iron foundry west of the Mississippi. The town holds a number of festivals in summer, including a Highland Heritage Festival in mid-July to honour the descendants of those who settled here in the 1850s.

Situated halfway down the Grand Staircase, Zion NP is another stunning and unique physical landscape. The park is a majestic, massive and formidable place and aptly named by the Mormons. *Zion* is the Hebrew word for 'sanctuary' or 'refuge'. The place has been a shelter and home for people and wildlife for thousands of years.

The best approach is through the South Entrance. Zion NP showcases several giant rock monoliths like the Watchman (6,545 feet) and the Great White Throne (6,744 feet), massive 2,000-feet-high cream, pink and red sandstone cliffs, and the fertile green canyon bottom of the wild and untamed Virgin River. The canyon and cliffs demonstrate vividly its massive destructive power, with the river sweeping away a million tons of sand, pebbles and boulders every year from its canyon into the Colorado River. Like Capitol Reef, the oasis environment of Zion attracted prehistoric Indians and, much later, the Mormons. The Southern Paiutes say that they have lived here since the beginning of the world, and they lived well in the Virgin Valley, hunting the many animals and gathering food and living materials from the abundant plant life. They still gather plants in the park. The self-sufficient Mormons had plentiful water for irrigation, growing corn, vegetables, fruit and tobacco, and they grazed livestock in the valleys and on the mesas.

The Zion Human History Museum is full of interest and the Pa'rus Trail and Riverside Walk make good strolls along the side of the Virgin River. There are longer and more strenuous walks too. Be aware that from late March to the end of October shuttle buses operate along the 6-mile length of the

Zion NP: the southern entrance; the canyon of the Virgin River; walking in Zion canyon, to the exclusion of private cars. About 2.5 million people visit Zion every year.

Zion Lodge is open all year round. Reservations are advised. Ring the Lodge on 1-888-297-2757. Otherwise St George (see Chapter 6) is a good place to stop before returning to Las Vegas or Salt Lake City on I-15. Either way you drive across the southeastern edge of the Great Basin, a physical environment in stark contrast to the Colorado Plateau.

6

Rim to Rim

Northern Arizona

This exhilarating drive circumnavigates Grand Canyon, the largest crack in the world's land surface. Passing through forest and desert, it combines magnificent views of the natural splendours of both rims of the Canyon with the fantastic man-made land and water landscapes created by the building of the Hoover and Glen Canyon Dams.

St George and Pipe Spring NM are memorable tributes to the Mormons and the Paiute Indians, the descendants of whom still live on the mile-high Arizona Strip. The roads on the Strip and around the eastern side of Grand Canyon follow the trails blazed by the great Mormon pioneer and explorer 'Old Jacob' Hamblin. The eastern side of Grand Canyon lies within the Navajo Reservation – the largest Indian reservation in America.

The South Rim offers more splendid and inspiring views of Grand Canyon. They contrast markedly with those of the North Rim. After Grand Canyon Village the road goes south from the Rim through Ponderosa pine and grassy plains to Williams and I-40. Coming west, the drive traces part of Arizona 66, the longest remaining section of the iconic Route 66.

The last part of the drive cuts north from Kingman through the hot Mojave Desert to Las Vegas, the unforgettable city of excess.

Suggested start/finish:	Las Vegas
Length of journey:	About 850 miles; 8 to 9 days
Best time of year:	Late May to early October
	NB: North Rim of the Grand Canyon NP is open only at this time.
Weather:	Hot and dry, but well moderated in many places by altitude and forest. Clear skies and cold at night.

NB: Carry spare water and food and keep the tank topped up.

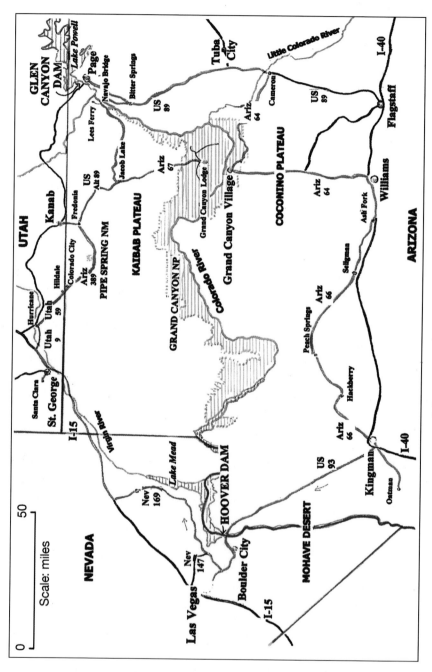

Map 7: Northern Arizona

Drive highlights

Las Vegas to St George (c. 110 miles)

I avoided the first 50 miles of I-15 North by taking Nevada 147 East from Las Vegas to North Shore Scenic Drive and then going north on Utah 169 to Overton. This alternative route goes through the Lake Mead National Recreation Area, created by the building of the Hoover Dam in the 1930s. This massive artificial landscape is one of blue water and sky separated by brown desert. The showpiece Lake Mead covers 247 square miles and it is America's largest man-made reservoir. Not only is it a gigantic watering hole for many kinds of wildlife, but it is also one of America's biggest human playgrounds – some 9 million people go there each year to swim, fish, boat and water-ski.

Lake Mead flooded a very extensive area of Anasazi settlement along the Muddy River, but not all of it was lost. The Pueblo Grande de Nevada in Overton stands on part of this prehistoric site. Part of the ancient pueblo (town) has been restored and pottery, baskets and items of turquoise jewellery put on display.

Twelve miles north of Overton, you reach I-15 which leads you across part of the Mojave Desert to St George in Utah, settled by Mormons in 1861. Everywhere they went the Mormons found the early going hard, but they endured in the wilderness and built towns that even today retain distinctive features of their Mormon origins. St George is one such place. It is a good overnight stop with an historic town centre and modern services.

St George's gleaming white, fortress-like church was the first Mormon temple in the American west. Nearby is the huge tabernacle, with red sandstone walls and a tall, slender white spire. The construction of these and other public buildings took years to accomplish. Thousands of Mormons worked on the sites either one day in every ten or in stints of forty days a year. Tithes given to the church in the form of grain or cattle were used to pay for wages and materials. The temple alone cost $1 million. Within easy strolling distance of temple and tabernacle are other buildings of the same period – the old red-brick county courthouse, jail house, opera house, a school, Judd's Store and many homes, including one (the Woolley Foster Home) believed to have sheltered polygamists and one which was the winter home of Brigham Young. Everywhere is highly manicured and free of litter and graffiti.

Brigham Young wintered in St George because its warm 'Dixie-like' temperatures helped his rheumatism. His home here contains many of his personal possessions. Open to the public, its guides still talk about him in hushed, reverential tones as they proudly show you around his house. You get the feeling that Brigham Young is listening in from a nearby room.

Statue of Brigham Young and (inset) his winter home in St. George, Utah

Three miles west in Santa Clare is another Mormon house, once the home of 'Old Jacob' Hamblin, a great explorer and coloniser of the Grand Canyon country, a renowned Indian peacemaker, and friend of Brigham Young and John Wesley Powell. In 1862 Hamblin became the first white man to ride round the rims of Grand Canyon. The roads I used in this drive to traverse the Arizona Strip and the eastern end of the Canyon follow the trails he blazed on horseback. Hamblin was also called 'the Buckskin Apostle'. He always spoke slowly and quietly to Indians, who listened in great awe. When he finished a sentence the chief repeated it, and then everybody gave a solemn grunt. Hamblin was trusted by the Paiute and the Navajo. Hamblin's house stands in its early frontier setting, built robustly of red sandstone and Ponderosa pine and designed to repel hostile Indians. Inside, the furniture and belongings give a fascinating glimpse of domestic Mormon life on the frontier 150 years ago.

St George to Kanab (c. 90 miles)

Continue north for 18 miles on I-15 and then turn east on Utah 9 to Hurricane and then take Utah 59 to Fredonia. The road leaves the Mojave Desert and climbs the western edge of the Colorado Plateau. Continue through the small settlements of Hildale and Colorado City, where it is said some Mormons still live in polygamy. Utah 59 becomes Arizona 389, once a rough wagon road used by Mormon pioneers. A huge stretch of land wedged between Grand Canyon to the south and the Vermilion Cliffs to the north now stretches out before you. This vast and lonely area is called the Arizona Strip. I was advised not to go off-road to try to look over the Canyon's North Rim. It is no place for a rental car. Terrain, weather and distance are adverse and there are no services. Rental car insurance does not cover mishaps on dirt roads.

Bronze plaque, old Mormon Trail on the Arizona Strip

Halfway to Fredonia you reach Pipe Spring NM, located on the Kaibab Paiute Indian Reservation. One of the few places in the Strip where water is always available Indians have used the spring for thousands of years. A statement on a wall inside the Visitor's Centre written by a modern Paiute spells

129

out for you the 'lifeway' of his tribe, a perspective intimately bound up with nature and the spirit world. Nature is sacred and all natural things are connected to one another. It is a world view in conflict with the mindset of modern man. It reads:

> *This land is the home of the Kaibab Paiute people. This is the place of our origin. We were brought here by Coyote in a sack. This is where my Sehoo (umbilical cord) is buried; it is my connection to this land. It is the place from which I will make my leap into the spirit world.*

Here too are the substantial remains of a Mormon settlement set up by Brigham Young in 1870. Impressed by the reliable water supply and lush grasses of Pipe Spring, he saw it as an excellent place to keep the swelling number of cattle tithed to the church by Mormon settlers in southern Utah. The ranch had orchards, gardens, corrals, cabins and a dugout and it was protected against Indians by a strong fort, its sturdy walls enclosing the main spring, a courtyard, living accommodation, a cheese room, and a telegraph office which was the first one in Arizona. Beef, butter and cheese from Pipe Spring fed Mormons in St George while they built the temple, tabernacle and other public buildings. The ranch cowboys also did stints of work there.

The fort had other purposes as well. In the later nineteenth century, when federal agents tried to stamp out polygamy, Mormon wives and children were left there by their fleeing husbands. Later on, the road past Pipe Spring was dubbed the 'Honeymoon Trail' when it became a popular overnight stopping place for Mormon couples travelling from the Arizona Strip and the Little Colorado Valley to the temple in St George to 'seal' their marriages in time and eternity. Early Mormons saw marriage as a sacred institution, even though many were polygamists. Brigham Young had 27 earthly wives. He was 'sealed' to some 50 other women to live with them in eternity after they died, and to another 150 who were in heaven already.

I continued on to Fredonia and then went 7 miles north on US Alt 89 to Kanab. Powell wintered here in 1871 and met with Brigham Young and Jacob Hamblin. In 1870 Hamblin had reoccupied the Mormon fort built here in the mid-1860s in order to do missionary work amongst the Indians. When Powell got here, the little town had a defensive square formed by a stockade and log houses, wide streets and quarter-acre plots each filled with fruit and shade trees, vines, corn and potatoes. It had a school, a meeting place and a ballroom. One of Powell's men wrote that the town had a thrifty air and per-

Pipe Spring NM, exterior and interior of the Mormon fort

fectly ordered government. 'Not a grog shop, or gambling saloon, or dance-hall was to be seen,' he said.

A century later, the magnificent scenery around Kanab made it one of Hollywood's most important locations for Westerns. Over 100 such films have been made at 'Utah's Little Hollywood' since filming began in the area in 1924. Have coffee at the historic Parry Lodge and look at the photographs of John Wayne and the scores of other famous actors and actresses who made films around Kanab and stayed at the motel. Stroll along to the Free Movie Museum, which has remnants of sets from Western films stored in a back yard. The barn and homestead sets used in the final shoot-out in Clint Eastwood's *The Outlaw Josey Wales* are here, still complete with their portholes and crosses. The area around Kanab also has places where abandoned and forgotten film scenery still stands. Details about this and accommodation can be obtained from Kanab Travel Information Centre, on 801-644-5033.

My wife and I have an amusing memory of our short time in Kanab. The

Parry Lodge, Kanab, exterior and interior

Homestead, and (inset) *The Outlaw Josey Wales*, Kanab

motel proprietor was fond of a little black pig which was totally oblivious to all the reprimands and admonishments his master made about his errant behaviour. It trotted everywhere, doing its own business. We kept our door firmly closed!

Kanab to Page via US Alt 89 (c. 207 miles)

This is a terrific part of the drive, but a long day if a booking cannot be made at the Grand Lodge, Grand Canyon North Rim (ring Forever Resorts, 877-386-4383 toll free). The Kaibab Plateau is covered in Ponderosa pine, blue spruce, Douglas fir, quaking aspen and lush meadows. It has many big-game animals and over 200 species of birds. President Teddy Roosevelt used to hunt mule deer and mountain lion here. In 1906 he created a National Game Reserve to protect the area's magnificently antlered mule deer, but hunters continued to shoot other wild animals. Lacking predators, the mule deer multiplied, depleted their natural food supplies and then died from mass starvation. Unintentionally, the great conservationist Roosevelt had caused an ecological disaster. Today the Forest Service keeps a strict control on hunting, deer herds and food stocks.

Commemorative plaque to Teddy Roosevelt, Arizona Strip

The huge domed limestone Kaibab Plateau is the highest land on the Arizona Strip, a massive buttress nearly 9,000 feet high that forces the mighty Colorado River to make a huge southward meander in its westward course across northern Arizona. Streams flowing into the Colorado from the Kaibab erode its plateau edges and form thick fingers of land which stick out into the Grand Canyon. They make splendid viewpoints.

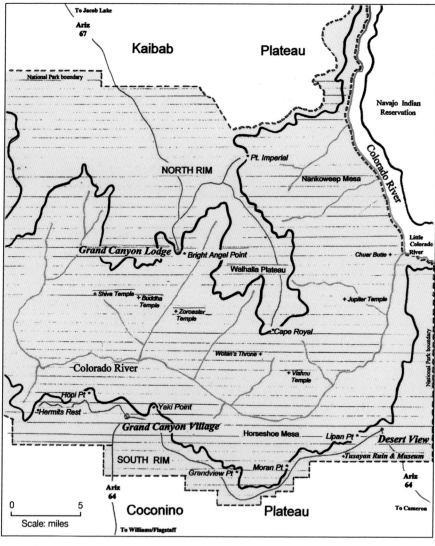

Map 8: Grand Canyon NP

In summer the Visitor Centre at Jacob Lake provides good information about the virgin wilderness here. The 45-mile drive south along Arizona 67, America's first Scenic Parkway, to the North Rim of the Grand Canyon NP is praised as the most pleasant short drive in America. Open only in the summer, it has some small lakes and lovely meadows with many grasses and wildflowers. Quaking aspens, with their white bark and green and silver leaves trembling in the breeze, stand out well against the forests of pine, spruce and fir. Grand Canyon Lodge itself has excellent vantage points. The self-guiding half-mile walking trail to Bright Angel Point is definitely worth the effort.

So is the 58-mile trail called the Cape Royal Scenic Drive which includes some of the most photogenic spots on the whole of the North Rim. Point Imperial stands at 8,803 feet above the river and desert, the highest point on the Arizona Strip. From here on a clear day you can see the Vermilion Cliffs to the north, Navajo Mountain to the northeast, the Painted Desert to the east, and the Little Colorado Canyon to the southeast. A plaque embedded in a piece of rock at Roosevelt Point makes plain how conservationist Teddy Roosevelt felt about the Grand Canyon:

> *Leave it as it is. You cannot improve on it. The ages have been at work on it, and man can only mar it. What you can do is to keep it for your children, your children's children, and for all who come after you, as the one great sight which every American … should see.*

At Cape Royal you gaze across one of the widest parts of the Grand Canyon. Beyond South Rim are the snow-peaked volcanic San Francisco Mountains, 70 miles away.

The Grand Canyon landscape so far has taken 5–6 million years to form. The views are incredible. Great walls, cliffs and amphitheatres have been cut into white, buff and red limestone and sandstone rocks. Red, green and purple shales and siltstones form aprons of crumbling slopes between the harder rocks. Erosion and weathering continue, wearing down the huge Colorado Plateau into mesas, and then buttes and spires, and finally into flat ground. Vivid in colour, these mighty rocks still crowd the Canyon – some nearly as high as North Rim itself. Many are named for the great gods, temples and palaces of ancient cultures. Majestic!

Jacob Lake to Page is another exhilarating drive. The road drops down several thousand feet from the cool green Kaibab Forest to the hot dry desert of the Colorado River and Marble Canyon. The windscreen is full of glorious

Bright Angel Point, North Rim, Grand Canyon NP

Erosion and weathering, colour and depth on rocks at North Rim

136

Vishnu Temple, North Rim

Angel's Window, Cape Royal Point,
North Rim

red cliffs, blue sky and white clouds. The Vermilion Cliffs are said to contain all the shades of red, including the colour of blood. Look high into the sky to see if you can glimpse any condors, recently reintroduced into the area. With 9-foot wingspans, these giant vultures can fly at 80 miles per hour.

US Alt89: Vermilion Cliffs, northern Arizona

The Dominguez-Escalante Interpretive Site, about halfway between Marble Canyon and Jacob Lake, is another little piece of the jigsaw of the Spanish explorations in the Southwest. In 1776–77 the two padres, along with eight other men, left Santa Fe in New Mexico to try to find a northward land route to California. Their purpose was much the same as that of the Spanish soldier, de Anza, who had done this the previous year when he marched soldiers and settlers from Tubac (southern Arizona) to San Francisco to establish a fort and a mission there. The two padres had great difficulty finding a way across the Colorado River, succeeding finally at a place called El Vado de los Padres (The Crossing of the Fathers), very near where the river enters Arizona. This historic crossing is now lost beneath the waters of Lake Powell, a fact much bemoaned by historians and conservationist opponents of the Glen Canyon Dam. The Interpretive Site marks a point on the return journey of the two men back to New Mexico, their expedition a failure due to winter snows in Utah and a serious shortage of food.

As you near Marble Canyon, look for some huge rocks at the base of the Cliffs which in the 1930s were used as homes by people who so loved the area that they decided to stay for a while. Just before the small settlement of Marble Canyon, take the turn pointing to the small historic district of Lees Ferry. At the river's edge you can see for yourself the break in the canyon wall where early Mormons crossed the Colorado into north central Arizona and marauding Navajos and Utes splashed north to raid early Mormon villages. In 1872 a Mormon, John D. Lee, started a ferry here. He was a cordial and generous host to John Wesley Powell's expeditionary party, who wintered in the area in 1871–72, but he met a bad end. In 1877 he was shot by a firing squad for his part in the massacre of gentiles in a wagon train crossing southern Utah during the 'Mormon War' of the late 1850s. Today the ferry is redundant, replaced by Navajo Bridge just a few miles downstream.

Navajo Bridge is a good place to view Marble Canyon. Look to see if there are any condors on the cliffs below the bridge. Glen Canyon Dam upstream controls the water in the canyon and the Colorado River moves along placidly. Not so in Powell's day. The river plunged for 65 miles over sixty or more boulder-strewn rapids and dropped 480 feet in its surge through the canyon. Powell and his men shot the white water but had to portage four times and lower their boats on lines six times in order to progress.

At Bitter Springs go north to Page on US 89. Just after this turn, stop at the roadside before you drive through a great cleft in the red Echo Cliffs above you. Enjoy the almost aerial views of Marble Canyon and the Vermilion Cliffs to the north and northwest. In summer the Navajo have some roadside jewellery stalls which are worth seeing.

US 89: Navajo trader near Bitter Springs

Once beyond the Cliffs, you enter the massive and superb man-made landscape of Glen Canyon Dam and Lake Powell. Red sandstone cliffs and gorges and their many reflections in the lake separate the blues of sky and water. The water stored here is vital to 20 million people throughout the Southwest and in parts of Mexico. The lake is 186 miles long with a shoreline measuring nearly 2,000 miles. Despite strong opposition, it has drowned for ever the once beautiful Glen Canyon and 96 of its side canyons. Sadly too, the great plumes of smoke from the coal-burning power plant on the Navajo Reservation mar the scene, polluting not only the reservation but the entire area, including Grand Canyon.

Coal-burning plant, Navajo Indian Reservation, Arizona

Glen Canyon Dam was the last of the great dams built across the Colorado River. Its building was bitterly contentious. In 2000 a contributor to a Public Broadcast Service (PBS) programme said, 'Next to nuclear power, dams are the biggest Faustian bargain that mankind has struck with nature. They have allowed us to settle places that could not be settled otherwise. They have created an outstanding amount of wealth. On the other hand they have had a terrible environmental impact.' Frank Waters, an Arizonan conservationist, deplored the fact that 'the Colorado itself … is no longer a river of mystic beauty and sublime terror. It is virtually a cement-lined irrigation ditch from source to mouth'. He added that the great wilderness of the American west was the spiritual heartland of the nation and that spiritual and aesthetic values must be weighed more in the balance when Americans propose projects to destroy the wilderness to meet the economic needs of the country's growing population. The argument carried weight. No more dams have been built across the river.

Glen Canyon Dam with Lake Powell in the background

Page began its life as the work centre for the dam and the lake. Now it is the tourist centre for a scenic wonderland. Recently voted one of the best 100 small towns in America, it deserves a two-night stay. There are some exciting things to do in and around Page: for example, a boat trip to Rainbow Bridge NM, a sacred religious site of the Navajo, or a short drive to Horseshoe Bend where the blue and green waters of the Colorado River make a spectacular 270° turn a few miles south of Glen Powell Dam.

In Page in June 2010 the newer motels proved expensive, so I looked for older, more modest accommodation. I noticed that rooms in 'Bashful Bob's Motel' were only $39, but that none were available. Nevertheless, I enquired at the office if the owner knew anywhere else at a similar price. Bashful Bob

Horseshoe Bend, near Page

beamed at me, saying that a cancellation had just been made and so he had a room to spare. He told me the man's name. He was a photographer from London. Did I know him? No I said. I did not live there and anyway the city had millions of residents. We got on with the business of signing in, but Bob could find neither a registration card nor a door key to the vacant room. We abandoned these matters and he led me along a line of rooms, trying to unlock doors with his bunch of master keys. When he finally unlocked a door, I stepped into the biggest motel accommodation I have ever stayed in – a huge, well-furnished lounge with a fully equipped kitchenette, two bedrooms, a separate shower and toilet, hallways, plenty of storage room and a front and a back door. I said he must have made a mistake over the price. He assured me he had not. I promptly booked a second night. The next morning Bob knocked on my door. He had a lady with him and introduced her as the guest I had been waiting for. My first thought was that $39 must also include a female companion, but the lady quickly perished the thought. Bob apologised profusely and led the lady away, feverishly trying other doors with his bunch of spare keys. He managed to open a door and I never saw the lady again. I shall never forget Bashful Bob, a nickname he said derived from his schooldays. I thought Forgetful Bob's Motel might be a more accurate name for his business, but Bob was kind and generous and unforgettable!

'Bashful Bob's' Motel, Page

Page to Grand Canyon Village, South Rim (c. 140 miles)

The road from Bitter Springs to Cameron along the base of the Echo Cliffs is the line of Hamblin's old trail linking the Mormons in Utah with the many thousands of Mormons who settled in central and eastern Arizona. In summer this is a very hot, dry place to be. Some Navajo Indians live beneath the cliff line, occupying Western-style prefabricated single-storey houses or mobile homes. Television aerials are commonplace and 4x4 vehicles the favoured means of transport. A careful look amongst the buildings reveals some traditional Navajo homes – the round or six-sided hogans made of logs or stone with their doorways all facing east. The Navajos revere the sun and these openings ensure that it is the first thing they see when they get up each day.

At Cameron, once an old-style trading post but now much modernised with a motel, petrol station and grocery store, you leave Hamblin's route and take Arizona 64 to Grand Canyon South Rim. The road crosses the Little

Colorado River and passes the Navajo Tribal Park, where I wandered around the Indians' stalls and looked down into the deep gorge of the Little Colorado River. Beyond this point the road rises from the desert to the cooler Coconino Plateau, studded with pygmy forests of juniper and Pinyon pine. Desert View is the highest point on the South Rim (7,438 feet). You get a spectacular view of the Colorado River being forced southwards by the massive limestone Kaibab Plateau, re-establishing its western course once this huge, resistant obstacle no longer blocks its path.

Desert View, South Rim, Grand Canyon NP

From the top of the stone Watchtower there is a 360° panorama almost as good as the views from Point Imperial. This high tower is symbolic of those built by the Anasazi in this vast region. The Hopi Indians, descendants of these prehistoric people, believe that their ancestors once lived below the surface of Grand Canyon but ascended to the earth's surface by climbing through a hole (a simpapu) in the canyon floor. Inside the Watchtower they have painted an image of their Snake Dance, a tribal prayer for rain so that they can grow their crops in this very arid land. Nearby is the ruin of an Anasazi pueblo called Tusayan, inhabited around AD 1200. Hunting wild game, gathering seeds and nuts from the plants around them, and growing corn, beans and squash in small deep holes in stream beds, these Stone Age people managed to survive the harsh climate here, at least for a little while.

It was here in 1540 that the Spanish captain Garcia Lopez de Cardenas, a member of the Coronado expedition seeking gold and treasure in the Southwest, became the first white man to see the Grand Canyon. He found no way to cross and was forced to turn back. A report of his discovery did say that he had open views across the Grand Canyon, and this places him somewhere between Desert View and Moran Point. Even now the Canyon remains an almost invincible barrier to north-south movement. You walk, or go by mule, or fly.

Beyond Moran Point as far as Grand Canyon Village the North Rim dominates the scene. It is at least 1,000 feet higher than the South Rim. But here, at various viewpoints, you understand why one writer described Grand Canyon as 'the house of stone and light'. Colours change constantly as sunshine, clouds and thunderstorms alter the light and shade in the Canyon. It seems mysterious, sublime and eternal. For people to propose building roads and railways through the Canyon, or that it be flooded to make a reservoir, is outrageous.

Sun, cloud, rain, light and
shadow, South Rim,
Grand Canyon NP

145

Sunset, South Rim, Grand Canyon NP

South Rim accommodation at Grand Canyon needs early booking (ring Xanterra Parks and Resorts, 888-297-2757 toll free, or 303-297-2757). Otherwise go to Tusayan, 7 miles south of Grand Canyon Village, or 60 miles to Williams on Arizona 64 South.

Williams is named for a well-known early nineteenth-century fur-trapper and mountain-man based in this area. The town was first put on the map by the Santa Fe Railroad, especially when it built a spur line to the Grand Canyon in 1909. In the 1930s it became one of the many small towns of America on Route 66.

Route 66: America's iconic road (Williams to Kingman, 126 miles)

America's first paved transcontinental highway Route 66 was 2,400 miles long, linking Chicago to Los Angeles. The road is hugely significant in the history and heritage of the American Southwest. In *The Grapes of Wrath* John Steinbeck called it the 'Mother Road', the road to California for hundreds of thousands of despairing farmers escaping the 'Dust Bowl' of the Great Plains in the 1930s. Post-war affluence spawned another great era of American restlessness as huge numbers of people took to the motor car to drive America. Dubbed the 'Main Street' of America, Route 66 was famous for its diners, hot-dog stands, ice cream parlours, fruit stalls, petrol stations, garages, camp-sites and motels. As early as 1946 Nat King Cole was urging Americans to 'get your kicks on Route 66'. Cruising along Route 66 became a national pastime, symbolising the new freedom and independence that paved roads and cars gave to more and more Americans.

The road was decommissioned after the construction of I-40. Its famous shield was removed from the roadsides. But it was not forgotten. Nostalgia for the road is growing. The Williams Main Street Association, for example, encourages motorists 'to take a step back in time' and 'cruise the loop' of streets in the town which display vintage Route 66 signs. In 1999 the road's historic importance was recognised by Congress in its ten-year Route 66 Corridor Preservation Programme, an initiative directed by the NPS. The longest remaining stretch of the original Route 66 is in Arizona. It is 140 miles long and in good condition. To get to it, go west from Williams on I-40 to Ash Fork, leave the freeway on Arizona 66 and head for Kingman through Seligman, Peach Springs and Hackberry, places where nostalgia for Route 66 still lingers.

Hackberry General Store, Historic Route 66

The road parallels the old Santa Fe Railroad. The quiet rural landscape is one of clean air, blue skies, snow-topped mountains and open, grassy plains.

You may glimpse deer, antelope, elk, prairie dogs and coyote. Some years ago now, I paid a small fee to the Indians of Peach Springs to drive across their reservation down to the Colorado, a place that Powell first saw in 1869. This was an exciting mini-adventure all on its own. It is the only place I know in the whole of the 277 miles of the Grand Canyon where you can park at the river's edge. Just beyond Peach Springs the road drops down the Grand Wash Cliffs, the western edge of the Colorado Plateau, and you re-enter the Mojave Desert. The stretch of road to Kingman is now designated a National Scenic Byway.

Kingman is a railway town and former gold-mining centre which became the main stop on the Arizona section of Route 66. Like Williams, it is trying to re-create something of the atmosphere of the good old days. Beale Street is the heart of the old shopping district. In Andy Devine Avenue the Visitor Centre is worth a look. Opposite is Mr D's, a diner with an original front and interior, which takes you back to the 1950s.

Mr D's Diner, with (inset) a James Dean cut-out, Kingman, Arizona

Route 66 once went through Oatman and Goldroad to Toppock on the border between Arizona and California. A gold-mining centre a century ago, Oatman became a ghost town with delapidated iron and wooden buildings creaking in the wind and wild burros wandering about the streets. Clark Gable and Carol Lombard spent their honeymoon night at the two-storey adobe Oatman Hotel. In more recent times the town has provided locations for Hollywood films such as *How the West Was Won*, *Foxfire* and *Edge of Eternity*. It has become a bit of a tourist hotspot.

Kingman to Hoover Dam and Lake Mead (75 miles)

Hoover Dam is north of Kingman on US 93, once a three-lane and dangerous road in the glare of the Mojave Desert sunshine, but thankfully now a double carriageway.

Hoover Dam and Lake Mead provide a great finish to this drive. Like Glen Canyon Dam and Lake Powell, they are magnificent man-made landscapes against the blues of water and sky. They were America's first projects to harness and control the immense natural power of the mighty Colorado River itself. They store water for irrigation and urban and industrial use, produce hydro-electricity, provide huge recreational areas for humans and offer precious habitat for wildlife.

US 93 drops down the side of Black Canyon to Hoover Dam. You can park in one of the free areas and walk across the top of the dam to the Visitor Centre. Alternatively, drive to it across the dam and park there. It has an excellent interpretive display of the dam and a film about its construction. The dam and the giant lake behind it were the last great work of Dr Elwood Mead, a man with a worldwide reputation for his work on water conservation and irrigation schemes. Lake Mead honours his name and work for ever.

The vision, planning and execution of an enterprise of this magnitude blows the mind. It gives credence to the saying that Americans 'do the difficult today and the impossible tomorrow'. From the viewing platform it is hard to say otherwise. At this spot the untamed Colorado once roared its way through a canyon 1,000 feet wide with sheer walls rising 1,250 feet from the riverbed. Before the dam construction could begin, a town for the workforce had to be built (Boulder), miles of road and rail links to the dam site laid down, and a 220-mile-long power line erected from San Bernardino in California to supply electricity. The river had to be diverted through four enormous tunnels drilled into the canyon sides, and the work site protected from flooding by two cofferdams. Over 9 million tons of rock had to be excavated, including all the loose rock on the sides of the canyon.

The federal government quite rightly honours the work of the ordinary man, epitomised by the statue of the 'high scaler' in front of the main public buildings at the dam. Men of great nerve, courage and fortitude, the high scalers worked all day in dust, summer heat and winter cold, slung from ropes hundreds of feet in the air, drilling holes and filling them with dynamite, clearing away loose rock and excavating the canyon sides for fixing the structures which had to be placed against the rock walls to build the dam. Some 400 men worked in this job for over two years. Seven men fell to their deaths.

'High Scaler' sculpture, Hoover Dam

Dam building started in 1931 and finished in 1936, one year sooner than planned. The dam itself consists of 215 concrete blocks built in vertical columns, all keyed together and grouted. The biggest blocks, on the upstream side of the structure, measure 60 feet square. Two of the four tunnels were converted to supply water through the four intake towers to turbines in the power plants built at the base of the dam. The remaining two were made into overflows or spillways. Over 4 million cubic yards of concrete were used, enough to build a skyscraper taller than the Empire State Building or to pave a 3,000-mile, two-lane highway from San Francisco to New York.

The dam stands on a base 660 feet wide, towers 726 feet high above the river, and supports a main highway across its crest which is nearly a quarter of a mile long. On average it generates about 4 billion kilowatt hours of hydro-electric power a year to consumers in Nevada, Arizona and California. Behind the dam the Lake Mead shoreline extends some 800 miles, penetrating 110 miles up the Colorado River and 35 miles along the Virgin. It stores some 35,200 million cubic metres of water, which is equivalent to two years of water flow along the River Colorado.

Hoover Dam in action *(Courtesy of the BLM)*

Once back in the car, drive up the other side of Black Canyon, stop at the viewing point for another look at Lake Mead and, if you have the time, visit the small desert town of Boulder. Built by the federal government as a model community for the dam workers, it has well-planned streets and buildings and is said to be the only city in Nevada without gambling dens and casinos.

As you drive back to the brash neon colours, extravagant air-conditioning and bountiful oasis of Las Vegas, you know now the secret of its survival and prosperity in such a hot and inhospitable place as the Mojave Desert.

7

Indian Country

Four Corners

Four Corners rivals the High Country and Grand Canyon in the drama of its natural and human landscapes. Monument Valley is the world's iconic image of the American Southwest. The towering sheer, smooth sandstone walls of Canyon de Chelly are stupendous and truly memorable. The Navajo NM in northeastern Arizona, Mesa Verde NP in southwestern Colorado, and Aztec Ruins NM and Chaco Culture NHP in northwestern New Mexico together make Four Corners foremost in America for the rich diversity of its archaeological remains of the Anasazi Indians.

Moreover, the Four Corners region has the largest concentration of modern Indians in the nation. Much of this drive lies within the reservations of the Navajo and the Hopi, who remain proud of their own heritage and culture. This drive offers the chance to visit their tribal centres, attend some of their annual events and ceremonies, appreciate their native arts and crafts, and understand something of their beliefs and ways of life which are alien but vulnerable to an all enveloping and threatening contemporary American culture.

Suggested start/finish:	Phoenix, Arizona
Length of journey:	1,420 miles; at least 9 to 10 days
Best time of year:	April to October
Road altitudes:	Generally between 4,500 and 7,000 feet
Weather:	Warm to hot summers and moderate to cold winters, depending on altitude.
	Rainy months are July, August and September; snow in winter.
Time:	NB: Between March and November clocks on the Navajo Reservation go forward one hour. The rest of Arizona does not make this time adjustment.

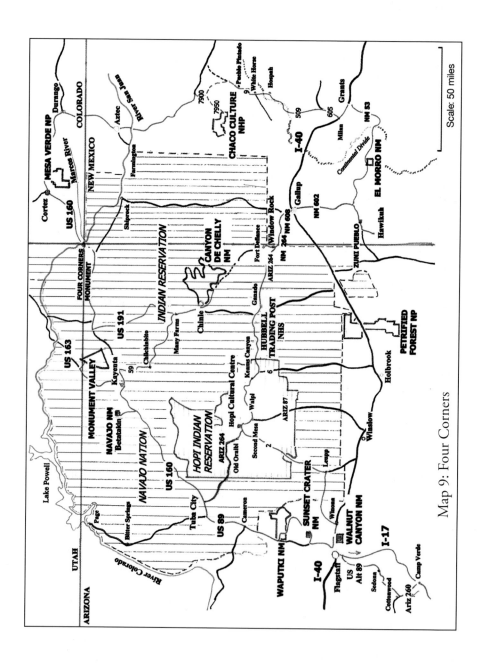

Map 9: Four Corners

Drive highlights

Phoenix to Flagstaff (c. 140 miles)

Go north from Phoenix through a fringe of the Sonora Desert, a natural landscape ravaged by urban sprawl and human litter. Rougher, hillier country follows and then come the Verde River, the Mogollan Rim which sharply defines the steep southern edge of the Colorado Plateau, the glowing red rocks of Sedona, and the volcanic, snow-capped San Francisco Peaks sacred to the Hopi and the Navajo.

Leave the freeway at Camp Verde, take Arizona 260 West to Cottonwood, and then US Alt 89 to Sedona and Flagstaff. At Sedona great sandstone buttes with names like Cathedral Rock, Courthouse Butte and Bear Mountain tower up to 2,000 feet above the town. Park the car and take a hectic and bumpy Pink Jeep ride into the mountainsides. Browse in the classy art galleries and boutiques of Tlaquepaque, a building styled on an eighteenth-century colonial Mexican village. Sit outside, have a drink and a bite to eat, and take in the town's lovely ambience. Blue sky and sunshine last nearly all the year round. Then continue north, driving up the Mogollan Rim through the colourful rocks and mixed forest of Oak Creek Canyon to Flagstaff, nearly 7,000 feet above sea level.

For me Flagstaff enjoys the best physical location in Arizona. People come here to ski in winter and to escape the lowland desert heat in summer. It is no backwoods town. The central area is highly commercialised (Santa Fe was once part of old Route 66), but its pleasant side streets are lined with attractive houses and trees. The railway is busy, the sounds of horns and sirens evoking scenes in Hollywood films. It has the Lowell Observatory, a university, a fine orchestra, a renowned Festival of the Arts in July and August, and the Museum of Northern Arizona with displays of the natural and human history of the area. There are many motels and restaurants.

Flagstaff to Kayenta (c. 180 miles)

The Flagstaff area has three prehistoric Indian sites associated with the Sinagua culture living here some 700 years ago. The Sinagua were heavily influenced by the Anasazi and they traded with them and the Hohokam in southern Arizona (see Chapter 8). These very interesting and diverse sites need only small detours on the road to the northeast and are worth doing.

Walnut Canyon NM, 13 miles east of Flagstaff on I-40, is a deep, winding gorge with firm pathways leading past scores of cliff dwellings high up on the canyon sides, some of which you can enter. Some remain blackened by fires which burned centuries ago. The Indians harvested many plants and hunted game in the canyon and farmed on the mesas above. The winters are hard, and to imagine living here in the snow and mist as a Stone Age Indian is difficult given our modern sedentary and pampered lifestyles. Although the Sinagua vanished from the archaeological record around 1400, an interpretive board at Walnut Canyon makes an extraordinary statement about a present-day Hopi's empathetic comment on the contents of a Sinagua grave. Twelve wooden wands were buried here with a Sinagua man. They were carved and painted to resemble hands, hoofs and other shapes. Puzzled archaeologists asked the Hopi about these objects. The Hopi not only knew what the wands were used for but described the ceremonial society to which the Sinagua man belonged. I think that is astounding: modern Indians still communicating with their Stone Age forebears!

Sinaguan cliff dwellings, Walnut Canyon NM, Flagstaff, Arizona

The loop road for Sunset Crater NM and Wupatki NM is signposted about 18 miles north of Flagstaff on US 89. The dramatic volcanic landscape of Sunset Crater was made by eruptions in 1064. There is a one-mile self-guiding loop trail around the base of the 1,000-foot cinder cone. The volcanic eruptions and the wetter conditions of the time encouraged the Indians to farm the Wupatki area. Today it is dry and desolate, but 700 years ago the land was capable of sustaining a multi-storeyed building of 100 rooms as well as small single dwellings. The 36-mile loop road itself is a pleasant scenic drive, passing through forests of Ponderosa pine, Pinyon pine and juniper, grassland and high desert.

US 89 enters the Navajo Nation Tribal Reservation near Gray Mountain. On both sides of the road the weathered bare rocks glint red, vermilion, lavender, yellow and brown in the sunshine. They are part of colourful badlands known as the Painted Desert. Pass through Cameron, cross the Little Colorado River, and after 16 miles go east on US 160 towards Tuba City. The tracks of dinosaurs some 180 million years old can be seen along a turn-off three miles from the junction. Tuba City began as a prehistoric Indian site and later was occupied by Mormons. It is now a tribal and trade centre for the Navajo and the Hopi. Baskets, pottery, woven goods and silver products are on sale. There is a motel there, Tuba Motel (602-283-4545).

The Navajo Nation Indian Reservation is huge, embracing over 25,000 square miles of land, mainly in northeastern Arizona but edging into Utah and New Mexico. It is America's largest Indian reservation and the Navajo are America's largest tribe. The Navajo run their own social services and police force and work hard to diversify the tribal economy, create jobs and raise living standards. The reservation earns millions of dollars a year leasing its rich reserves of oil, gas, coal and uranium to American companies, but the reservation is short of jobs and many live and work beyond its boundaries. Conservative Navajos rue the day when such agreements were made, because coal-mining and power stations have blighted the landscape of their homeland, which they call 'the land of the beautiful rainbow'.

Most Navajos on the reservation are found in its towns – Tuba City, Chinle, Fort Defiance, Window Rock, Shiprock and Gallup. You meet them in places like shops, motels, gas stations and public service facilities. Their life and work are a far cry from what they did in the past, but reflect their great and enduring ability to adjust to their changing circumstances. Today most Navajos live in American-style prefabricated housing and mobile homes, but often with their more traditional homes or hogans nearby. They wear cowboy hats, jeans and boots, love rodeos, drive 4x4 trucks, watch American television, shop in supermarkets and enjoy coffee and hamburgers. But they remain proud of their history and culture.

NAVAJO HISTORY AND CULTURE

Navajo roots lie in Canada and Alaska. They were hunters, fishermen and plant gatherers. They drifted south, arriving in the Southwest about 500 years ago. Since then they have been influenced by the Hopi and other pueblo Indians, the Spanish and the Americans, learning how to raise crops, keep sheep, ride horses and use guns. By 1850 Americans were eyeing Navajo lands and demanding army protection. Fort Defiance was built there. In 1863–64 Kit Carson and a volunteer army forced the Navajo from their homelands and the 8,000 Navajo who surrendered or were captured were made to walk 300 miles under harsh discipline to a reservation in New Mexico. Hostile Navajos, however, continued to attack the Americans. In 1868 the Navajo agreed with the Americans to return to part of their homeland and live on a reservation tending sheep and goats. Soil erosion and over-grazing led in the 1930s to the federal compulsion of drastic livestock reductions on the reservation and the end of the Navajo dream of a pastoral idyll.

Remarkably, Navajo culture remains strong and vibrant. Navajos still speak their own language as well as English. Few are Christian. The Navajo are a major force in the life of the Southwest and vocal in the fight to educate Americans to a better understanding of Indian values and traditional ways of life. They are not descendants of the Anasazi, whose archaeological remains are everywhere across their reservation, but, together with the NPS, the Navajo are the modern protectors of these fragile and precious sites.

Navajo tradition says that the tribe has emerged from an underworld of chaos and disharmony into a natural world of order and beauty. Changing Woman and the Holy People have taught the Navajo how to live in harmony with each other and the natural world. The hogan is the very centre of Navajo life, a home, a refuge, and a sacred place for the ceremonies they have to perform to achieve this harmony. The rituals are complex and involve chanters (singers), songs, prayers, sacred bundles and dry-paintings (sand-paintings). They address matters like poor health, bad luck, witchcraft, puberty and marriage. Going on all year round, these sacred ceremonies are performed inside hogans. They are private affairs and are not seen by the general public. Children also learn their tribal traditions and customs at reservation schools.

Navajo women say Spider Woman taught them to weave and they have become world famous for their distinctive rugs and blankets. Their best work reflects the brilliant colours and geometric shapes of the natural landscapes of their reservation. Teec Nos Pos and Ganado are good places to see weavers at work. Navajo men are unsurpassed silversmiths. Their necklaces, bracelets, pendants and buckles are often inlaid with polished turquoise. Turquoise figures in many Navajo legends and the people like to wear it as an outward sign of their personal well-being.

An hour's drive northeast along US 160 from Tuba City brings you to Arizona 564, the road to Navajo NM. From the Visitor Centre you walk out for half a mile along the high spur of the Sandal Trail. To your left you look down on the salmon-coloured Tsegi Canyon, where springs along the canyon walls provide small oases and patches of greenery. Not quite sure where to look your eyes suddenly focus on the Anasazi ruins perched high on a sandstone ledge inside a huge cave, every detail clear in the morning sunshine. It is a magical moment! Binoculars are a real bonus.

Betatakin ruin, Navajo NM

Betatakin is a Navajo word meaning 'ledge house'. The opening in the canyon wall is 452 feet high, 370 feet across and 135 feet deep. The great pueblo (Indian village) has 135 connected rooms and is built of stone masonry, mortar and timber. It has one small square chamber called a kiva, a place for religious ceremonies and rituals. Between 100 and 150 people lived here. Tree-ring dating puts the Anasazi occupation between 1250 and 1300. Why the people stayed such a short time is uncertain.

Experienced walkers wanting to walk to the ruin must turn up early at the Visitor Centre. Group size is limited and it is first come, first served. The trail is two and a half miles and 700 feet down below the canyon rim. Essentials are a gallon of water, food, sun hat and good walking gear. The uphill return is hard going: the altitude here is around 7,000 feet. (Ring 928-672-2700 for more information.)

Continue northeast to Kayenta on US 160. Along this part of the road coal is being stripped from Black Mesa, a hideous scar on the Navajo homeland. In Kayenta there is the Best Western Wetherill Inn (928-697-3231) and Holiday Inn (928-697-3221). Overnight accommodation in Monument Valley is improving, but prices are high. The View Hotel (435-727-5555) is brand new and stands within the Valley, with every room looking out on the iconic landscape. Gouldings Lodge (435-727-3231) makes similar boasts.

Monument Valley is 24 miles north of Kayenta on US 163. In 1938 it was virtually unknown when John Ford and John Wayne made the Western film *Stagecoach*. Many Navajo lived there with their livestock. Sheep, wool and weaving were essential to daily living. Rugs were made for use as clothing, bed blankets and saddle blankets and they were sold to pay for food. Today some Navajo still live there amid the serene red landscapes under a vivid blue sky. The great mesas, magnificent buttes and fragile rock spires are now world famous. For many, Monument Valley is the defining image of the Southwest. These remnant pieces of landscape are all that is left of a huge plateau once standing thousands of feet above the present valley, now almost eroded away by water and wind. These huge monoliths have names like the Mittens, Totem Pole, Three Sisters and Big Hogan. You can drive through part of the

Monument Valley, northern Arizona

monument and see, for example, John Ford's Point (one of Ford's camera locations) and the hogans of the few Navajo who still live there. It is best to hire a Navajo guide who will take you where you could not go by yourself.

Kayenta to Chinle (c. 140 miles)

Retrace your route to Kayenta and keep north on US 160 for about 20 miles. Turn south on County Road 59 to Chilchinbito, Rough Rock and Many Farms, and then take the main road to Chinle. Thunderbird Lodge, owned by the Navajo, stands right next to the Canyon de Chelly. It is a good place to stay if you can get in. There are other motels in the town.

It has been said that Canyon de Chelly NM is one of the loveliest and most serene places in North America. Sheer, smooth sandstone walls rise dramatically to 1,000 feet above green, fertile canyon floors. Here you can see hogans, cottonwoods, patches of farmland and orchard, and livestock. One of the great heartlands of the Navajo, this canyon is a tribal monument and private ground with little free public access. Like Mesa Verde NP, the canyon bears human imprints made over many centuries, especially those of the prehistoric Anasazi and the Navajo who came here in the seventeenth century. From a distance the Anasazi multi-storeyed living complexes in the cliff alcoves seen here are visually even more spectacular than those in the Navajo NM. The darkest moment in the canyon's long human history occurred in the very cold winter of 1863–64 when Kit Carson and mounted soldiers attacked the canyon, destroying its wells, crops and animals and forcing the

Anasazi pueblo,
Canyon de Chelly NM

Navajos to surrender and make their 'Long Walk'.

Much of the monument can be seen from overlooks on paved roads along the canyon rims. Binoculars are very useful. The only place where you are free to walk down into the canyon is at White House Overlook and this is well worth doing. The self-guiding trail drops 500 feet down the canyon wall and leads along the canyon floor to White House Ruin. A stone pueblo of some 60 rooms, the cave recess was inhabited by about 100 Anasazi between 1060 and 1275. Otherwise, to see the canyon bottom you need to pay a Navajo guide to take you down there. This is a great experience. Vivid blue sky, Anasazi pueblos in the sides of majestic red cliffs, yellow cottonwoods and sparkling streams present a grand panorama as the jeep splashes through the canyon's streams.

Stream and cottonwoods, Canyon de Chelly NM

Chinle to Cortez (c. 155 miles)

Drive north on US 191 and then east on US 160. These roads penetrate a lonely but historic area. In the 1860s many Navajos fleeing from Kit Carson's invading army crossed this area to hide in the valleys of the Colorado and its tributary the San Juan. Six miles after Teec Nos Pos you will see signs to Four Corners NM and Navajo Tribal Park. Make sure you get there in the daylight so that you can see the great stone plaque on the ground which shows the exact point where four states meet – Arizona, New Mexico, Colorado and

Utah. There is no other such point in America. Straddle the point, place a hand and a foot in each of the four quadrants and be photographed in four states at once! In 2010, however, the monument was closed for refurbishment and I could not even glimpse the new look planned for it.

Continue on US 160/491 to Cortez. The growing popularity of Mesa Verde NP has seen the town blossom as a tourist centre and it is now an obvious base from which to discover the spectacular development of Anasazi culture in the Four Corners area.

ANASAZI CULTURE

The Anasazi people first lived on the Colorado Plateau some 1,400 years ago. Nomadic at first, they then lived in one-family pit-houses clustered in small villages mainly on mesa tops. They grew corn, beans and squash, hunted game with spears, and gathered wild plants. In the early phase of their cultural development they made finely woven baskets. This 'Basketmaker' period dates roughly from 550 to 750.

As numbers grew, the Anasazi became centred in three main parts of the Plateau – at Kayenta, Mesa Verde and Chaco Canyon. Archaeologists tell us that the Anasazi believed themselves to have risen from the underworld to the earth's surface through a hole (simpapu) in the ground. They had a deep respect for nature and its spirits and sacred places. Their farming methods and knowledge of pottery and other crafts improved alongside their planning, building and architectural skills. By 750 the Anasazi were starting to live together in multi-roomed stone houses above ground called pueblos. Their pit-houses became kivas, places where family-based clans performed their religious ceremonies. Large kivas were built as well, serving the whole pueblo community.

The 'Pueblo' period peaked between 1100 and 1300, but by the end of this period they were drifting away from their traditional homelands. Over-population, depleted soil and game and drought were some probable causes for this widespread desertion. The great pueblos of Kayenta, Mesa Verde and Chaco Canyon became the first ghost towns of America. The Anasazi dispersed to mesas in northeastern Arizona and to the Zuni Mountains and Rio Grande areas in New Mexico, where their culture was later attacked but not destroyed by Spanish landowners and priests. Today Indian tribes like the Hopi and the Zuni still live in pueblos, speak pueblo languages, practise pueblo religious rituals and dwell on lands their gods tell them are at the centre of the world.

Anasazi Culture at Mesa Verde NP, a World Heritage Site

Almost everywhere you drive on the Colorado Plateau there is evidence of the prehistoric Anasazi – the 'ancient ones' as the Navajo call them. Nowhere is this evidence more in place than at Mesa Verde NP. Some 4,000 archaeological sites have revealed weapons and tools, pit-houses, remains of foods and animals, clothes, pottery, basketry, kivas and stone-built multi-storeyed pueblos with many rooms built on hill tops and in the sides of cliffs – all evidence of continuous settlement and cultural development here from 600 to 1300. In 1978 UNESCO chose Mesa Verde as a World Heritage Site because it was so well conserved and uniquely exhibited the life and work of ancient man. It has become the most visited archaeological area in North America.

Mesa Verde NP

Mesa Verde NP is 7 miles east of Cortez on US 160. The Spanish words mean 'Green Table', an apt description of the area which is a large, high table-land covered in Pinyon pine and juniper. Its north side is well over 8,000 feet high, the land sloping gently away to cliffs along the southern perimeter overlooking the Mancos River Canyon. The park road is steep and winding with good overlooks to the north and over the river. Park Point, for example, the highest part of Mesa Verde at 8,571 feet, has splendid panoramic views of the Four Corners region. Far View Visitor Centre is a must, its film presentation *Anasazi* depicting the fascinating history and lifestyle of the people who once lived here. The comments in the next paragraphs only give a small taste of what you can see in this great National Park.

Far View Sites Complex is an example of an open village on the mesa top. Settled in about 900, this site housed 500 people two hundred years later. A century later the people were moving from the tops of the mesa to homes tucked away in the sides of the cliffs. The building complexes included spaces for living, ceremonials and social gatherings, trade and barter. Spruce Tree House, the third largest cliff dwelling at Mesa Verde, was home to about 100 people. It is approached down a steep path which takes you through a landscape of plants well known and used by the Anasazi. You walk back some 800 years in time. Spruce Tree House has 114 rooms for daily living and 8 kivas. One of the kivas is roofed and you can descend into it by a ladder and stand in a place where important religious ceremonies and rituals once occurred. Here the priests would invoke the spirits to bring rain, ensure good crops and make hunting successful.

Spruce Tree House, Mesa Verde NP, with insets of a roof-less kiva and the ruins of multi-storied Anasazi houses

Cliff Palace is the largest and most famous cliff dwelling in America. When found by Americans in 1888 (the Ute Indians had known about it well before then), it still had complete clay pots and stone tools, and ashes in the fire pits. It has over 200 rooms and 23 kivas. Most impressively, the pueblo blends with the encompassing world of nature, its masonry walls running parallel or at right angles to the slopes of the cave and stopping short of the line where water drips down from the alcove's rim. Visits to Cliff Palace, Balcony House and Long House are seasonal, the ticketed ranger-led tours requiring some driving, walking and climbing up and down steps and ladders. Check the details at the Far View Visitor Centre before you buy your ticket.

Cliff Palace, Mesa Verde NP

Cortez to Grants (New Mexico) (c. 250 miles)

Across the border in New Mexico the small and attractive town of Aztec boasts the excellent Aztec Ruins NM. The ruins are the substantial remains of a large Anasazi pueblo built three storeys high and housing between 500 and 700 people. The Great Kiva is a stunning reconstruction evoking an Anasazi ceremonial and social gathering place. It is unique: as far as I know there is no other restored great kiva in existence. It was the People's First House, the place where all their clans celebrated the story of their origin, their emergence from the Earth's navel symbolised by the *simpapu*, the hole in the floor of the kiva.

Great Kiva, Aztec Ruin NM, New Mexico, and (inset) inside the Great Kiva

About 55 miles further south in New Mexico is Chaco Culture NHP. Leave US 550 some 3 miles beyond Nageezi. County Roads 7900 and 7950 lead to the park. These roads are rough and the park barren and secluded. But in Chaco Canyon Anasazi life and culture at its zenith surpassed even that of Mesa Verde. Some archaeologists praise Chaco Canyon as the Rome of the Puebloan world, its huge towns and great kivas the equivalent of European palaces and cathedrals. Chaco acted as the ceremonial, political and economic centre for about 75 outlying communities spread across 40,000 square miles of the San Juan Basin. Four hundred miles of roads connected Chaco to its outlying settlements. Fires and reflective slabs of rock provided a signalling system for messages and intelligence.

The Visitor Centre is the first port of call, to watch its film presentation of the Anasazi and to get a map of the Chaco Canyon and its pueblo sites. A loop road connects short walking trails to six of the eleven pueblos in Chaco Canyon. Pueblo Bonito, the largest one of all, stands on the northern side of the canyon, facing south for winter sunshine. Aligned with the cardinal points, the building stood on stone rubble and clay mortar foundations. When it was finished it had 800 rooms, 32 small kivas for family and clan use, and two circular and part-subterranean great kivas. There was also a large

Pueblo Bonito as it may have appeared in the early A.D. 1100s

Pueblo Bonito and (inset) architectural plan,
Chaco Culture NHP, New Mexico
(Courtesy of the NPS)

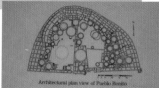

Architectural plan view of Pueblo Bonito

Anasazi houses and kivas, Pueblo Bonito

plaza and many storage rooms. One million sandstone blocks weighing 30,000 tons were used to build the pueblo. Over 200,000 pieces of timber for the floors and roofs were dragged 50 miles from the mountains west and south. The huge building complex exceeded 4 acres in size.

The road to Grants from Chaco Canyon NHP is a minor one and tricky to follow. Go back to County Road 7900 which goes south to Pueblo Pintado and White Horse. Keep south on New Mexico 509 to Hospah and Ambrosia Lake. The road is perched on the Continental Divide. It becomes New Mexico 605 during the final few miles to I-40.

Grants started out as a small railway town in the 1870s. It boomed as a mining town for uranium after the Second World War, but now it is growing as a tourist centre because of the attractive landscapes and significant prehistoric remains in the area.

Grants to Gallup (c. 145 miles)

The reasons for the widespread and total abandonment of the Four Corners region by the Anasazi remain mere speculation. Beyond Four Corners, however, some pueblos survive even now. Two of these areas are highlights of this drive – the Zuni Pueblo in New Mexico and the Hopi Reservation in northwestern Arizona.

About halfway along New Mexico 53 on the way to Zuni Pueblo, stop at El Morro NM. This is a spectacular sandstone rock formation and oasis. Pueblo Indians once lived here and in historic times the rock has been a refuge for many Spanish and American explorers and emigrants. A rather strenuous climb up and over the rocks leads you to the remains of a large pueblo, petroglyphs, a spectacular box canyon and good panoramas of the surrounding area. A gentler halfmile loop trail leads to the pool past many hundreds of carved names and signatures still visible in the cliff walls. Many are still readable, but they are fading away and the rock is losing its rare, hand-carved register of its unique human history.

Zuni Pueblo is the largest of the 19 surviving Indian pueblos in the Southwest and the last surviving village of the so-called fabulous 'Seven Cities of Cibola' sought by Coronado in 1540–42. But when the Spanish conquistador came here there was no gold or silver. He wrote that there were 'just seven little villages ... a total of five hundred houses ... very good houses three, four and five storeys high ... with some quite good apartments underground and paved (i.e. kivas)'. The Indians brought him gifts of deer and buffalo skins, poor blankets, some turquoises and a few bows and arrows. Archaeologists have found only six villages. Today they are consolidated into one settlement – Zuni Pueblo – which surrounds the old pueblo called Halona, one of the two villages actually named in Coronado's description of the Seven Cities of Cibola.

Like all the remaining pueblo settlements, Zuni has its own government, tribal constitution, police force, school district, radio station and tribe-owned businesses. The pueblo maintains strong links with its past through religious activities and other traditional practices which are sacred to the Zuni. Visitors are welcome, but they must obey tribal etiquette. For example, they must watch the religious dances from the rooftops, refrain from photographing them and keep out of the kivas. The dates and times of the dances are never published beforehand. The old Spanish mission building remains here and attracts tourists, but hardly any Zuni are Christians. Zuni are buried there, but no living Zuni enters the graveyard. The Zuni authorities hire other people to keep the place clean and tidy.

Old Spanish mission and graveyard, Zuni Pueblo

Twelve miles south of Zuni Pueblo is Hawikuh, the second village named in Coronado's diaries. It is a ruin now and only accessible to visitors with a guide from the Zuni Pueblo. Yet in July 1540 this was the place where Coronado and his men stormed Cibola. The painting by artist Nevin Kempthorne is a dramatic impression of the arrival of Coronado's expedition at the Zuni pueblos in 1540 and imagines the first time in history when the white man fought Indians in battle. The Indians were ready to fight. Warriors from other pueblos had come to help Hawikuw. This large, strong pueblo stood in a commanding position. Hundreds of men were inside the pueblo and many more were outside. Showers of arrows kept the Spanish cavalry away from the walls. Coronado, conspicuous in his gilded armour and plumed helmet, changed tactics and led an infantry charge against one of the entrances to the pueblo. He was knocked unconscious by stones thrown down on him, but his men won the day.

Coronado arrives at the Zuni Pueblos *(Courtesy of the NPS. Image of a painting by Nevin Kempthorne, Coronado NM)*

Gallup is the main trading centre for the Navajo and the Zuni Indians. There are 110 trading posts, shops and galleries here, mostly along Main Street (old Route 66) and Coal Street. Both tribes make intricate silver and turquoise jewellery. If time is available, a two-night stopover is well worth it. You might wish to consider the El Rancho Hotel, once frequented by famous film stars. Today the town is famous for its annual Inter-Tribal Indian Ceremonial held during the second week of August at Red Rock SP. The park provides a wonderful amphitheatre of sandstone cliffs for tribal dances, exhibitions of native arts and crafts, and a rodeo. Ring Gallup Convention and Visitors Bureau on 505-863-3841 or 800-242-2482 for more information.

Gallup to Hopi Reservation (Arizona) (c. 120 miles)
Northwest of Gallup on Routes 608 and 264 is Window Rock, the tribal

171

capital of the Navajo Reservation and the seat of government. The inside of the Council Chambers is shaped like a hogan. The small park nearby was one of the places where Carson held surrendering Navajos before their detention in New Mexico. The Navajo Code Talker Memorial celebrates the work of Navajo soldiers in the Pacific Theatre during the Second World War. The Code Talkers passed secret messages for the armed services speaking in Navajo, a language unknown to the Japanese, who were quite unable to break the codes used by the Indians – a failure which greatly helped the Americans to win the war in the Pacific.

The statue of a Navajo Code Talker, in front of Window Rock, Navajo Nation Indian Reservation, Arizona

The town is also the home of the Navajo Tribal Museum and the Navajo Nation Zoological and Botanical Park which includes animals native to the reservation and domestic ones important in Navajo culture. On the first weekend after Labour Day (1 September) the town hosts the largest Indian Fair in North America. Very popular, this includes a parade, a rodeo, a pow-wow, art and craft displays, and tribal songs and dances in native costumes.

Fort Defiance is just north of Window Rock. This was the storm centre during the war between the Navajo and the Americans in the 1850s and early 1860s. In 1863 it was Kit Carson's HQ while he was fighting the Navajo. The 'Long Walk' was a brutal shock to the Navajo: they lost their freedom and their homeland. In 1868, however, when the Americans allowed the Navajo to go back to part of their homelands, Fort Defiance became the first government town on the Navajo Reservation and the springboard for its future development. In the countryside all around there are many small Navajo settlements, often with six-sided hogans among the buildings.

Navajo settlement with hogans

The growing presence of white Indian traders on their reservation was an important factor in the revitalisation of the Navajo after 1868. These men encouraged the Indians to develop their weaving and metal-working skills to higher levels and sold their goods to Americans and people overseas. One of the most important traders was John Lorenzo Hubbell, who set up his trading post in 1876. The buildings remained in the hands of his family until 1967 when the NPS became both owner and operator.

A visit to the Hubbell Trading Post in Ganado, 26 miles west of Window Rock on Arizona 264, is a great experience. The house and trading post are little changed over the years. The store is full of tinned goods, sugar, flour, tobacco, rugs, blankets, saddles, harness, hardware, silver and turquoise jewellery, and many other items, all on counters, walls and ceilings in several rooms. The place seems steeped in the past and you feel you have stepped back in time. Navajos still trade here. You can too. My wife is the proud possessor of earrings and a necklace set in silver and turquoise, a silver bracelet made up of dancing Navajo children, and the tiniest silver and turquoise tea service you can imagine.

The Rug Room, Hubbell Trading Post NHS

The Hopi Indian Reservation

Continue west on Arizona 264 into the Hopi Reservation, much smaller than the Navajo Reservation and completely surrounded by it. The people and the place are amazing. They number only 10,000. In their own words they are 'intensely spiritual and fiercely independent'. Each of their 12 villages is self-governing and Hopis identify strongly with their own village and clan. Their villages have stood on the tops of three fingers of land jutting out from Black Mesa for hundreds of years. They are one of the world's oldest and most lasting cultures. And perhaps more successfully than any other Indian tribe they have protected their ancient teachings, traditions and ceremonies from the inroads of American culture, despite it being increasingly hard for them to do so.

HOPI HISTORY AND CULTURE

The Hopi believe that their Spider Grandmother led them out of subterranean underworlds where evil spirits lived by climbing through a hole in the ground into Grand Canyon. The Great Spirit, Muusau'y, told the Hopi where they could settle on the earth and the clans of the people searched for centuries to find it. The three mesas where the Hopi live now are the appointed place, the centre of the Hopi universe. Here they try to live in peace and harmony with nature and other people. The spirit world is paramount and eternal. Spirits are everywhere – in clouds, mountains, streams, trees, animals and plants. The spirits live in the sacred San Francisco Peaks. They act as messengers of the gods (kachinas) when they come down from the mountains between early spring and mid-July. Then, in the village kivas and plazas, Hopi men in costume perform various kinds of dances to please the spirits and persuade them to answer their prayers for rain, health and fertility when they return to the mountains. Parts of these dances are held in public at weekends during spring and summer for tourists to see. The famous Snake Dance, involving deadly rattlesnakes, is a dramatised prayer for rain.

Don Talayesva, a Hopi Sun Clan chief in the late nineteenth century, said, 'When I am too old and feeble to follow my sheep or cultivate my corn, I plan to sit in my house, carve kachina dolls, and tell my nephew and nieces the story of my life. Then I want to be buried in the Hopi way. Perhaps my boy will dress me in the costume of a Special Officer, place a few beads around my neck, put a paho (digging tool) and some sacred corn meal in my hand, and fasten inlaid turquoise to my ears. If he wishes to put me in a coffin, he may do even that, but he must leave the lid unlocked, place food nearby, and set up a grave ladder so that I can climb out. I shall hasten to my dear ones, but I will return with good rains and dance as a kachina in the plaza with my ancestors...'

Like the Anasazi, the Hopi grow corn, squash and beans in tiny plots of ground, the seeds poked in deep holes by sticks. The Hopi also keep livestock, including sheep, cattle and horses, which they first saw when the Spanish came to the Southwest. Like all pueblo Indians, the Hopi revolted against the Spanish in 1680, an event remembered to this day. The Spanish failed to Christianise the Hopi, who still speak a pueblo language as well as English. A respectful, reserved and private people, the Hopi have only recently welcomed visitors to their reservation. Visitors are asked to respect Hopi traditions and culture and not to take pictures of their dances in the plazas. Tourists are not allowed in the kivas.

Tourism in the Hopi Reservation centres on visits to the Hopi villages on the three mesas, the public dance ceremonies and the sale of craft goods such as their distinctive black and yellow pottery, baskets, kachina dolls and silverware. The Hopi Cultural Centre on Second Mesa is well worth a visit and there are art and craft centres and trading posts across the reservation.

Keams Canyon is the reservation's agency and government town. (Keams Canyon Motel can be contacted on 602-738-2291). Nearby Kit Carson carved his name on Inscription Rock. Follow Arizona 264 West for 15 miles towards Polacca and then take a steep, narrow road to the top of First Mesa and the villages of Hano, Sichomovi and Walpi. Walpi is dramatically placed right at the end of First Mesa, connected to the other two places by a narrow neck of land only 15 feet wide. Its very old houses have been restored in breeze-block and stone, but they still lack running water, proper sanitation and electricity. Only three or four families live there all year round, but others come back frequently to take part in the ceremonies in the kivas and the plaza. It does have spectacular views of the Painted Desert and its sunsets. Guides give walking tours along the mesa top to Walpi.

Second Mesa is 10 miles west of First Mesa. The Hopi Cultural Centre (928-734-2401) is part-pueblo in style, the complex containing a museum, craft shops, a café and a motel, all owned and managed by members of the tribe. It takes bookings for motel reservations and gives information about times and dates for public performances of Hopi dance ceremonials. Old Oraibi, said to be the longest continually inhabited Indian settlement in America, is on Third Mesa. The village is old-style pueblo with a multi-level

Hopi hill-top settlements, Hopi Reservation, Arizona

living complex with rooms around a central courtyard. It has no entrances to it at ground level.

Hopi Reservation to Phoenix (c. 240 miles)

Go south on Navajo 2 to Leupp. You get excellent views of Old Oraibi and the three Hopi mesas and then panoramas of the Painted Desert. At Leupp take Navajo 15 to Winona and then I-40 West to Flagstaff and I-17 South to Phoenix. You have another chance to explore the invigorating Flagstaff area before dropping down the Mogollan Rim and returning to the warm Sonoran Desert.

8

Saguaro and Apache

Southern Arizona

The first part of this trip explores the Sonoran Desert in southern Arizona. Like the Anasazi, the Hohokam Indians established a pre-eminent civilisation in American prehistory, but it was in this desert, not on the Colorado Plateau. Some remains of Hohokam culture are still visible in Phoenix and at Casa Grande. In its natural state the Sonoran Desert is one of the most fertile deserts in the world, positively exuberant in its displays of plants, animals and birds. The best two places to experience it are the Saguaro NP and the Arizona-Sonoran Desert Museum. The saguaro tree logo is the international symbol for deserts.

The desert was also of interest to Spain well before the British colonised the eastern seaboard of America. In 1540 the Spanish conquistador Francisco Vasquez de Coronado crossed the eastern side of the Sonora Desert on his way north to find the treasures of the fabled Seven Cities of Cibola. Much later the Santa Cruz Valley was crucial to Spanish intentions to Christianise the Indians and make them into good Spanish citizens, and to develop an overland route to California to safeguard Spain's northern-most frontier in the New World.

The second part of the drive explores the extreme southeastern corner of Arizona. The Coronado NM is here. Bisbee, once a premier copper-mining area in Arizona, is now one of the state's compelling small towns. Tombstone is forever known as the place of the most famous shoot-out in American western history. Cochise and Geronimo, however, are as famous as Wyatt Earp and visits to the Dragoon and the Chiricahua Mountains and short walks at the Fort Bowie NHS leave no doubt about the American cavalry's problems when fighting the Chiricahua Apaches between 1860 and 1886.

Suggested start/finish:	Phoenix
Length of journey:	About 850 miles; 6 to 7 days
Best times of year:	Winter, spring, late summer and autumn
Weather:	A lot of sunshine and low relative humidity most of the year.
	In the winter days are mild and pleasant, but nights are cool.
	Gentle light rain with snow in higher places.
	In the summer, days are very warm – 100°F or more.
	Heavy thunderstorms in late June and July, often after strong winds and dust storms. More humid.
	Cooler temperatures in the mountains with seasonal rains.

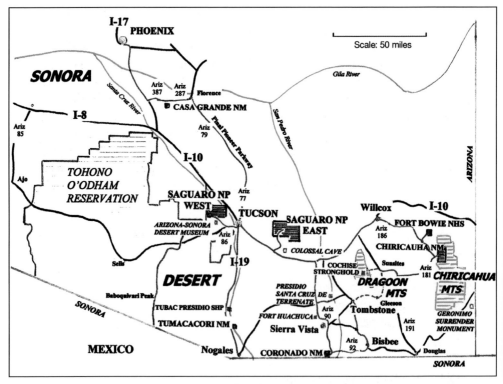

Map 10: Southern Arizona

Drive highlights

Phoenix to Tucson (c. 135 miles)

The modern expansion of Phoenix has smothered the natural desert and buried most of the physical remains of the seminal Hohokam culture of the American Southwest. Phoenix did not rise from its own ashes but from these prehistoric Indians who cremated their dead. Part of one important Hohokam site, however, has remained within the city's boundaries. Called the Pueblo Grande Museum and Cultural Park, it is a National Historic Landmark. Here is part of a prehistoric village completely surrounded by a great metropolitan city. The Stone Age stands side by side with modern America. The park includes a huge platform mound the size of a football field, a restored ball court and vestiges of a canal all linked by an interpretive trail. The well-appointed and very well-presented museum houses an enormous number of artefacts excavated in and around the site which show the daily life and work of the people who lived here. Meanwhile, planes fly in and out of Sky Harbour Airport, traffic buzzes along the nearby streets and freeways, and skyscraper buildings are visible in the distance.

Head south on I-10 to the junction with Arizona 387, turn east and then go straight ahead to the Casa Grande Ruins NM near Coolidge. The monument has several separate compounds, all part of the one village, with a ball court and plaza area which were the centre of community life. Each compound contained houses, courtyards, storage places and work areas – all hives of human activity. In the ball court players knocked a hard ball up and down using only their arms and hips in a game brought from Mexico, but the purpose of it unknown. The largest compound, however, has the biggest Hohokam building ever found. Called the 'Casa Grande' (Big House), it is

Old postcards showing artists' impressions of Hohokam life at Pueblo Grande and Casa Grande. (*Casa Grande postcard by courtesy of Smith-Southwestern*)

181

four storeys high, stands 35 feet tall and is hand-built from 3,000 tons of a sticky mud called *caliche*. The Ponderosa pine and white fir timber for the beams were dragged or floated from the mountains 50 miles away.

Today, the 'Big House' has a prefabricated roof over it to protect it from sun and storm. Debate continues about its real purpose. Suggestions are that it was a chief's house, a storage facility, a temple or palace, an administrative centre, or a mix of these things. Opinion now leans towards the idea that the Casa Grande was an astronomical observatory and calendar. Windows and doorways in the top storey of the building aligned with the sun or moon at particular times of the year, setting the religious and festive days in the annual calendar.

Casa Grande, Casa Grande NM, southern Arizona

As one drives south, the desert becomes more palpable. Go along the Pinal Pioneer Highway between Florence and Tucson which runs through a well-preserved but tiny piece of the Sonora Desert, its distinctive plants lining the road as far as the Santa Catalina Mountains. Tucson has boomed since the Second World War, but its centre is still small enough to walk round. Desert plants invade the streets. A mix of buildings reflects the city's past under Spanish, Mexican and American flags. There are some 50 motels and a good variety of restaurants and nightlife, some with patios and flamenco music and dancing.

THE HOHOKAM – IRRIGATORS OF THE SONORAN DESERT

The Hohokam lived well in the harsh climate of the Sonoran Desert for over 1,000 years. Their great zeal and practical ingenuity made up for the lack of metal tools, draft animals, wheeled transport, and stone and timber. They built villages like Casa Grande and Pueblo Grande and their settlements spread over 45,000 square miles of desert along the rivers of the Salt, Gila, Santa Cruz, San Pedro, Verde and Agua Fria. Amazingly they hand-dug 600 miles of canals with simple tools and much effort. The biggest canals measured 75 feet across the top and 50 feet at the bottom.

The Hohokam grew corn, beans, squash, cotton and tobacco in their irrigated fields. From the desert they gathered seeds and fruit from plants like the saguaro, mesquite, cholla and prickly pear. Altogether it is thought they harvested some 200 sorts of plants, even the creosote bush which they used as a medicine to reduce breathing problems. They hunted and fished for jackrabbit, quail, fish and turtle. From below their feet they took a multi-purpose sticky mud called caliche to build walls, seal roofs and plaster walls and floors.

They made distinctive 'red-on-buff' pots with line patterns and animal figures drawn on them with brushes made from hair or yucca fibre. Shells, gathered from the Gulf of California 200 miles away and carried back in shoulder baskets, were made into beads, bracelets and pendants exquisitely finished with decorations of frogs, birds and human figures. These decorations even appeared on small scraped and polished pieces of rock. These goods were used by the Hohokam, especially at their cremation ceremonies, but they traded them extensively across Arizona as well.

What became of the Hohokam remains a mystery. By AD 1450 their civilisation was gone. Did the exceptional floods and droughts of the fourteenth century ruin their canals, the very basis of their lives in the desert? Was it, as Pima legend says, that evil people gained control of the Hohokam and a widespread revolution amongst the Indians led to the destruction of their culture and way of life? The Pima and the Papago Indians are the modern-day descendants of the Hohokam.

Drives in the Tucson area

1. Saguaro NP (West), Arizona-Sonoran Desert Museum and Old Tucson (c. 50 miles)

Saguaro NP stands on both sides of Tucson. It protects and preserves the natural landscape and the wildlife of the Sonoran Desert. This drive concentrates on Saguaro NP West. (Its eastern part is best seen after a visit to Colossal Cave – see later.)

Saguaro NP West is best approached on Arizona 86 (Ajo Way), turning north after 5 or 6 miles on Kinney Road to a first stop at the Park's Red Hills Visitor Centre. Outside the Visitor Centre is the Cactus Garden Trail and a mile further down the Kinney Road a Desert Discovery Nature Trail – both good places to learn to appreciate this wonderful desert.

The Sonoran Desert can be a forbidding and hostile place. The summer heat is fierce; the land is parched; occasional thunderstorms bring dangerous flash floods. Spiny plants are everywhere – prickly pear, barrel cactus, fishhook and pincushion cacti, staghorn, and teddy bear cholla. It is a land of rattlesnakes, scorpions, tarantulas and Gila monsters. But the desert is unimaginably vibrant and exotic. Saguaros pierce the skyline, palo verdes splash the landscape with lovely yellows and blues, ocotillos produce bright red tips after a rainfall and, when the earth gets a good soaking, desert annuals cover the ground in swathes of flowers in glorious technicolour. The solitude is filled with the sounds of doves, red cardinals, Gambel's quail and cactus wrens.

Common plants of the Sonoran Desert

Postcard image of desert plants *(Courtesy of Smith-Southwestern)*

The giant saguaro is the most distinctive plant of the Sonora Desert. It only lives in Arizona and Mexico. It grows slowly and does not start to branch until it is about 75 years old. After 150 years it is mature, with a cluster of arms. Like the Joshua tree, it looks bizarre and unreal with a human-like appearance. When the saguaro is full of water its arms are uplifted, praising the desert. In times of drought its arms droop and the tree looks dispirited. The Papago Indians endow the saguaro with human feelings and see it as a sacred plant. Their New Year begins with the harvesting of the saguaro fruit, which they make into jam, syrup and wine.

The saguaro is a home and a food store for wildlife. Gila woodpeckers and golden flickers live in the trunk. They only use the hole once, making new ones for the next season. Other desert birds such as kestrels, warblers, cactus wrens, pygmy and elf owls, screech owls and purple martins use the abandoned holes which offer coolness in summer and warmth in winter. Red-tailed hawks and Harris hawks nest in the top of the tree. In early summer, as the saguaro's large white waxy flowers bloom and its fruits ripen, javelinas, coyotes, foxes and squirrels, ants and birds feast on the red pulp and black seeds.

A mature saguaro with nest holes

Beyond the two walking trails mentioned already the road now becomes part of the Bajada Loop Drive. This leads through one of the best stands of saguaro in the whole desert and, along the Valley View Overlook Trail, provides a superb view of a part of the 'basin and range' landscape so characteristic of the Sonoran Desert and the American Southwest generally. The Avra Valley (a basin) is full of sediments brought down by the streams from the nearby mountains (ranges). These sands and silts form cone shapes (alluvial fans) across the valley floor which join together to form bajadas. When the stream beds are empty they are picked out by blue paloverde, desert willow and desert lavender growing along their edges.

The Arizona-Sonoran Desert Museum, back along Kinney Road, has been called 'the most distinctive zoo in America'. Like the park, its display of desert plants is excellent but here there is a wonderful chance to see in safety all of the creatures of the desert's 'basin and range' country. Apart from the 1,200 species of plants, there are more than 300 kinds of birds and 200 kinds of animals in natural surroundings. See a raptor, mountain lion, bighorn sheep, coyote, rattlesnake and a Gila monster and live to tell the tale!

On the way back to Tucson there is the famous Old Tucson Movie Studios. The mock frontier town built there became the set for many films. John Wayne, for example, made four films there – *Rio Bravo, McLintock, El Dorado* and *Rio Lobo.* In 1995 a great fire destroyed the buildings, costume wardrobe and memorabilia associated with the many actors who worked there. Today there are new buildings and streets, but the studio's glory days have gone. There are tours of the site relating to old films, and actors still present shoot-outs and stunt shows for the public to watch.

2. The Santa Cruz Valley (c. 120 miles)

I-19 south from Tucson to Nogales on the border with Mexico leads through the Santa Cruz Valley. This valley enjoys a distinctive place in the state's history. The first seeds of Hispanic culture were planted here over 300 years ago by the black-robed Jesuit missionary Father Kino, called by one of his biographers 'the padre on horseback'. And it was from here in 1774 and 1775 that Juan Bautista de Anza set forth on his great overland expeditions to San Francisco. Three places in the valley have great interest in these respects – Tumacacori NM, the town of Tubac and the Mission of San Xavier del Bac.

Father Kino, the first great Jesuit missionary in southern Arizona

Father Kino worked with great zeal in the last 24 years of his life to establish Spanish influence here. He explored and mapped the Sonora Desert in southern Arizona, he baptised thousands of Indians and arranged regular visits to their villages by himself and other missionaries, and he located sites for missions like Tumacacori and San Xavier, personally driving cattle to them to try to ensure their economic survival. Tubac became a mission farm and ranch. But the desert was large and hard to cross. The Apache Indians especially were hostile and often raided the missions. Money to strengthen the missions was always in short supply. After Kino died, the opening of Spanish silver mines disrupted the life of nearby missions. The Pimans revolted in 1751, killing priests and destroying churches. In 1767 Charles III summarily banished the Jesuits from the Spanish Empire. The ongoing missionary work in southern Arizona was given to the Franciscans.

Tumacacori NM is at Exit 29 on I-19. The mission here is not on the Kino site. The Indian village was moved here after the Piman Revolt. The present church was built by the Franciscans between about 1800 and 1822. It is unfinished, the flow of money to all missions in southern Arizona having been cut off completely after Mexico declared its independence from Spain in 1821. The Franciscans finally abandoned Tumacacori in 1848, the Indian congregation moving the church furnishings to San Xavier del Bac.

Tumacacori became a National Monument in 1908. The church ruin remains substantial and impressive in a simple way. The self-guiding interpretive trail around the building and its grounds is a good short walk. The patio garden proves a real eye-opener. The missionaries had a huge knowledge of Sonoran plants, herbs, flowers and trees and made great use of them in the daily life of the mission. The museum has a good film and exhibits of daily mission life.

Tubac was southern Arizona's first presidio, built immediately after the Piman Revolt. Its second captain was Juan Bautista de Anza, born in Mexico but from a Basque family. In 1774 Anza led a military expedition west across the desert and crossed the Colorado into California, going north as far as Monterey, proving that there was a viable overland route to Spain's far northwestern frontier. In 1775 the viceroy of New Spain authorised Anza to take a party of volunteer soldiers and their families to settle San Francisco, build a fort and a mission, and thereby allow Spain to better defend its claim to California from Russia and England. The trail he took in 1775–76 is known today as the Juan Bautista de Anza National Historic Trail.

The diaries of both Anza and his Franciscan chaplain, Pedro Font, also give details of this prestigious occasion. The day before the start, mass was

Artist's impression of the
church interior during the
early 19th century.
*(Courtesy of the NPS,
Tumacacori NM)*

Tumacacori church mission

chanted and hymns sung to gain God's favour for this momentous journey.
When the cavalcade left the town it contained 240 people and 1,000 animals.
The red-coated soldiers held bannered lances and the friars wore blue robes
and leather sandals. Twenty-eight of the soldiers/settlers had their wives and
children with them, all recruited by Anza from ranches and mines in northwestern Mexico. Children made up more than half the party. Anza had 220
horses and mules as mounts for the soldiers, 140 pack mules to carry camp
gear, baggage, food, ammunition and gifts for the Indians. The 6 tons of food

included beans, flour, cornmeal, sugar and chocolate. In addition, 320 beef cattle were herded along as food supply on the way and to stock the land once San Francisco was reached. The journey took nearly six months and covered 1,200 miles. The route crossed both the Sonoran and the Colorado Deserts. Anza lost just one person, who died in childbirth, and three children were born on the trail. The expedition proved to be one of America's great adventure stories and it helped to bring profound cultural changes to California. An original piece of Anza's trail lies between Tumacacori NM and Tubac SHP. You can walk in Anza's footsteps! Today Tubac is an artists' retreat with many studios and galleries. It is both lively and relaxed and worth a wander around.

The mission at San Xavier del Bac is very much alive and well. Called 'the white dove of the desert', it is the most beautiful piece of Spanish colonial architecture in Arizona. Its resident congregation are Papago Indians whose

San Xavier del Bac Mission Church, Indian Reservation, southern Arizona

ancestors knew Kino when he arrived here in 1692. Two Jesuit churches were built at Bac, but this brick church is Franciscan, constructed in the 1780s and 1790s. The east tower was unfinished and remains so today. Like other missions, Bac suffered the consequences of the Mexican Revolution – the sale of its estate, no resident priests for many years, church decay and Apache depredations. The Franciscans finally returned to Bac in 1913, taking over a restored church painted white and more buildings, including a school. The buildings have been cared for ever since by priests and the Papagos. It is a must-see site in any drive around southern Arizona.

THE PAPAGOS TODAY

The Papagos now call themselves by a name from their own language – Tohono O'odham, which means 'desert people'. They live on a reservation which occupies some of the Sonoran Desert in southern Arizona. It covers part of their traditional homelands which used to stretch as far as the Lower Colorado River and south into northern Mexico. The O'odham speak their own language and Spanish.

The Tohono O'odham Reservation is the second largest reservation by area in America. Some 6,000–7,000 people live there, but many others reside in surrounding towns or even further away. The 50 or more small villages stand on both high and low ground, reflecting an old way of life when the O'odham lived on the better-watered slopes in winter and in the valley bottoms in summer when their crops were growing. Today the government has dug wells and the Indians no longer move from one village to another. Agriculture remains important and the tribe continues to excel in basketry. Some O'odham keep cattle. The reservation, however, depends on federal money to survive and most O'odham work on the reservation in hospitals, schools, clinics, utilities and transport. Its administrative centre is at Sells. Santa Rosa is the only other large community.

Most O'odham remain Catholic, but they retain their tribal legends, customs and traditions. Most of their villages have a small church or chapel, full of holy pictures and objects. They like religious processions and feast days and they make annual pilgrimages to Kino's burial place in Magdelana in Mexico. But the areas around the churches have stone crosses on pedestals, dance floors, kitchens and eating rooms. The churches are not simply a focal point for prayers, but also for dancing, eating and socialising. Nonetheless, Baboquivari Mountain remains the centre of their desert universe. It is the home of I'itoi, their Creator and Elder Brother, who still comes down among the people in times of great need. In recent times an old Indian said, 'I still believe in Jesus and the saints but I know too that when we drink the wine (of the saguaro fruit) and sing for I'itoi's help, the rains will always come.'

Tucson to Sierra Vista (c. 110 miles)

I-10 East beyond Tucson traces old stagecoach routes and follows the tracks of the Southern Pacific Railroad. The natural landscapes along this road are little changed from the old days. The Sonoran Desert begins to disappear. 'Basin and range' country continues, but the land is higher and cooler. The Santa Ritas, the Huachucas and the Chirichua – 'islands in the sky' –stick up from the desert reaching well over 9,000 feet, their slopes clothed in oak woodlands and pine forests. They are part of the Coronado National Forest. Yucca-dominated grassland and desert scrub fill the valleys between, the lowlands now part of the Chihuahuan Desert.

Colossal Cave, just north of Exit 279, is a huge limestone formation with numerous fissures, caverns and natural hallways. Early cave tours here sometimes lasted several days, the guide and visitors sleeping in dry subterranean river beds. Stalactites and stalagmites form weird and wonderful shapes – kings and queens, witches, organ pipes, even a pterodactyl if your imagination stretches that far! Hohokam artefacts have been found. Bandits and outlaws once holed up here, leaving behind blankets, canteens and empty gold bags. It is said that Virgil Earp once staked out the cave because he thought train robbers were inside. A body of a dead Apache was also found here. Or are these simply good stories to promote the business? On this same road is the access to Saguaro NP East. This part of the Park has bigger and much more mature saguaros and other cacti than the other part so do not miss it even if you visited Saguaro NP West.

Further along I-10, I turned south on Arizona 90 and made for Sierra Vista. Go east at the junction with Arizona 82 and drive to Fairbank. Here are the remains of the Presidio Santa Cruz de Terrante, an isolated Spanish fort in Apache country in the late 1770s. It must have been a tense posting for the soldiers and their families who were sent here. Even then these Indians were formidable enemies. The walls of the fort were not as high as planned. The bastion/gunpowder storehouse was incomplete and only a quarter of the barracks were finished. Only mud walls remain now, but an interpretive trail reveals the hardships suffered by these people, who endured here for four years. The San Pedro Riparian NCA all around the fort boasts 350 kinds of birds, 80 different mammals and 45 reptile and amphibian species. Its nature trail along a tree-lined path is worth a stroll.

In contrast to the Spanish presidio, Fort Huachuca, remains a key military installation even now. It was built in 1877 as a cavalry post to protect settlers and travellers in the San Pedro Valley from the Apaches, It had a good water supply and forest for wood and shade. Its defences were strong and its look-out point over the valley was excellent. In 1886 it was the advance headquarters during the final months of the campaign against Geronimo. Barracks and offices of that time still line the parade ground and the museum has a large collection of documents and photographs covering the history of this wild frontier.

Fort Huachuca, south-eastern Arizona

Sierra Vista has grown up as a service town around Fort Huachuca. Many retired servicemen live here. Sited on the eastern side of the Huachuca Mountain, the town has a mild climate and scenic views of the San Pedro River. Rodeos take place most weekends.

Sierra Vista to Tombstone (c. 80 miles)

Coronado NM is 20 miles south on Arizona 92 and then west along Montezuma Canyon Road. The monument stands in oak woodlands dotted with yucca, cholla and beargrass which bloom in late spring and summer. It commemorates the expedition led by the Spanish conquistador Francisco Vasquez de Coronado across the American Southwest between 1540 and 1542, the first major exploration here by a white man. The Visitor Centre contains some striking paintings of Coronado's expedition and a display of Spanish armour and weapons of the day.

The road continues for 3 miles to Montezuma Pass (6,575 feet). Steep and winding, it has tremendous views east and west. Looking westwards on clear days you can see the Santa Rita Mountains and even Baboquivari Peak some 80 miles away. I parked at the road summit and then climbed to the top of Coronado's Peak. Many of the words on the marker boards along the trail are taken from the diaries of a soldier who travelled with Coronado. At the top of the hill another great panorama awaits. You look out over the place where the conquistador and his soldiers, friars and Indian guides came marching out of Mexico and northwards into America along the San Pedro Valley. They sought the fabled Seven Cities of Cibola and fame and fortune. Two years later they returned. Dispirited and disconsolate, they had not found the treasures they had dreamed about.

Coronado expedition 1540–1542 *(Courtesy of the NPS. Image is a painting by Nevin Kempthorne. Coronado NM, southern Arizona)*

For 300 years or more the diaries of the expedition lay untouched and dusting in Spanish archives. Today, however, Coronado enjoys a good reputation with historians. His expedition was the very first one to record significant details of the landscape and its wildlife and the lives of the Hopi and Zuni Indians in the American Southwest. His captains also discovered the Grand Canyon and the Lower Colorado River.

Back on Arizona 92, it is less than an hour's drive to Bisbee, squeezed into steep-sided ravines in the Mule Mountains. In its early years it rivalled Tombstone for lawlessness, gambling and prostitution, but its mines were to bring it much greater wealth. By 1900 Bisbee was the largest place in Arizona

Territory. Mexicans, Germans, Italians, Irishmen, Serbs and Russians migrated there in large numbers, forming their own 'neighbourhoods' within the town. The story of the town is well told in the Bisbee Mining and Historical Museum in Copper Queen Plaza. Between 1875 and 1975 the town mined 8 billion pounds of copper, its massive operations paid for by the huge Phelps-Dodge Company.

Since its demise as a mining town, Bisbee has become one of Arizona's 'great little towns'. Its pleasant climate, clean air, Victorian buildings and friendly, relaxed atmosphere attract artists and artisans, dancers, writers, musicians, photographers and tourists. John Wayne stayed here once, in Room 10 of the Copper Queen Hotel. Who is this chap? He always seems to go where I go and get there first!

For me the town had two special attractions, and I do not include John Wayne! For $10 I had a 75-minute ride into the heart of Queen Mine. Kitted out with a miner's helmet, yellow PVC jacket and a miner's lamp with a five-and-a-half-pound battery, I rode a small train sitting astride a plank into the blackness of the mine. The train's main stop was at a huge opening 30 feet high and shored up by timber. Ledges led off to work places. When the guide turned off the lights, we were in utter blackness. In the early days there were no safety precautions and deaths were common. A miner's working life was

A Queen Mine adventure, Bisbee

195

reckoned at 15 years, if he was lucky. Six thousand men worked in the mine at its peak of operation, when there were 140 miles of underground tunnels. The ride was atmospheric and sobering.

Equally stunning is the great open-pit Lavender Mine, seen 1 mile south of Bisbee on Arizona 80. This is a gigantic man-made hole in the ground, and the miners dug out around 380 million tons of ore and waste in some 70 or 80 years of work. When the mine closed, it was 1.25 miles long, nearly a mile wide and 950 feet deep.

Arizona 80 goes north to Tombstone across a dreary creosote landscape called Goose Flats. The town's silver-mining boom in the late 1870s lasted less than a decade, the mines becoming swamped by water. Yet it has become better known than Bisbee because of its defining moment in 1881. And that is all it was: 30 shots in as many seconds, a deadly event in the bitter rivalry between the Earps and the 'cowboys', a gang of rustlers, outlaws and gunfighters. Wyatt Earp survived unscathed, Doc Holliday was grazed, and Morgan and Virgil Earp were seriously wounded. Frank and Tom McLaury and Billy Clanton died, and Ike Clanton and Billy Claiborne ran away. The 'Gunfight at the OK Corral' became the most famous shoot-out in history. With this one event Tombstone secured its place in the history, myths and legends of the Southwestern frontier.

Today in Tombstone, grim-faced moustached men in their black hats and long black coats, and mean-looking cowboys in their coloured shirts and bandanas, jeans and leather boots, all stride along Allen Street, spurs jangling on the wooden sidewalks, pushing open the doors of Big Kate's Saloon (known as the Grand Hotel in 1881) or the Crystal Palace, calling people to an afternoon shoot-out. And every day in the tourist season, at 2 o'clock, the Gunfight of the OK Corral takes place again. Throughout the year various other 'celebrations' of Tombstone in the 1880s are acted out in the town as well – 'Territorial Days', 'Wyatt Earp Days', 'Vigilante Days', 'Rendezvous of Gunfighters' and 'Helldorado Days'. Fact is overwhelmed by myth and make-believe.

The real shoot-out settled nothing. The 'cowboy' gang was determined to get revenge on the Earps. Virgil was later ambushed and suffered crippling injuries. Morgan Earp was killed by an unknown assassin. Wyatt Earp believed this was Frank Stilwell. Shortly afterwards he killed Stilwell and was charged with his murder by the sheriff of Cochise County, John H. Behan, himself an adversary of the Earps. The national press got hold of the story, asking what right a law officer had to shoot down someone in cold blood. Earp had his defenders, but his reputation was badly tarnished. He left Tomb-

A modern-day shoot-out in Tombstone, Arizona

stone in March 1882, never to return. Since that time a fierce debate has raged: was Wyatt Earp hero or villain? The bookshops in Tombstone will provide evidence for both points of view. But the re-enactments of the Gunfight at the OK Corral continue to be simple morality plays: good triumphs over evil. It is profitable civic business!

Tombstone to Willcox (c. 140 miles)

This is a long drive through some lonely places. It explores the heartland of the Chiricahua Apaches, the tribe which fought the American army so valiantly between 1860 and 1886. I started early with a full tank, food and water.

The Dragoon Mountains

Leave either Sierra Vista or Tombstone and go to Gleeson, Pearce and Sunsites. Just beyond Sunsites on Arizona 191, turn west to Cochise's Stronghold in the Dragoon Mountains. Throughout his ten-year war against the Americans in the 1860s, the Dragoons were the main base for Cochise. In fact he had two strongholds there – one on the west side of the mountains, the other on the east. The 8-mile unmade road to get to the eastern base of these mountains is itself tough going. As you get closer to the Dragoons, their impregnability becomes obvious. No medieval fortress could compare. High look-out points over the valleys, huge cliffs and boulders, and narrow valleys and rocky defiles defied attackers. In 1871, when Cochise agreed to peace, he dictated that the Dragoons, the Chiricahua Mountains and the Sulphur

THE CHIRICAHUA APACHES

Coronado encountered the Apaches during his search for the Seven Cities of Cibola. They had drifted to the plains and deserts of America from Alaska and northwestern Canada sometime between AD 1000 and 1500. They lived in small groups related by blood, but combined together in bands against their enemies. Nomadic hunters, raiders and warriors, the Apaches traded and stole from other Indians and resented and opposed with force the growing presence in their adopted homelands of the Spanish, Mexicans and Americans. The band which occupied the extreme southeast of Arizona was known as the Chiricahua, and they proved extremely resistant to their enemies, including the Americans who found both Cochise and Geronimo determined and ruthless opponents.

From childhood, boys and girls were trained in hardship and survival. Chiricahuas could cover 50–60 miles a day, on foot if necessary. They knew how to find water and food in the desert and they cached guns, ammunition and other supplies for use along their trails. The band's heartlands were the Dragoons and the Chiricahua Mountains, which hid their presence and movement from their enemies. They also lived in the Sierra Madre in northern Mexico.

Cochise, chief of the Chiricahua, fought a ten-year war against the Americans which cost the federal government $40 million. But Cochise knew that he could not fight them forever or stop the influx of white people into his homeland. In 1871 he accepted a reservation for the Chiricahua, but insisted that it must embrace the tribe's homelands. It was so until Cochise died, but then the Americans forced the Chiricahua to move to the San Carlos Reservation north of the Gila River, where they were expected to mix with other Apache bands and to learn to become farmers.

Geronimo was not a chief, but he was the most formidable leader of small groups of renegade Apaches who wanted to be free to live as they had always done. He hated San Carlos and said that farming was for women. He led raids in Arizona, New Mexico and Mexico. A great resistance fighter who symbolised his tribe's resistance to the Americans, he was intelligent, amazingly mobile in mountains and deserts, and fought until he was over 60 years old.

Springs Valley must be the heart of his reservation. No soldiers were to be there and Tom Jeffords, a man he trusted, must be the Indian agent. From his eastern stronghold Cochise could see across all of his reservation. He died there in 1874, but the whereabouts of his grave is unknown.

The Chiricahua NM is directly west from Pearce along US 191 and Arizona 181. As always the Visitor Centre is the first port of call. The monument protects what the Apaches called 'the land of the standing up rocks', a fantastic area of rock spires, huge stone columns and massive rocks perched on ridiculously small ones. Here, too, is an exotic world of plants and animals which reflect those in the Sierra Madre. Some rocks have names like Organ Pipe, Sea Captain and Punch and Judy. The winding 8-mile drive up Bonita Canyon to Massai Point (6,870 feet) passes many features of the monument. The point has commanding views of the Chiricahua homeland and gave Cochise another perfect vantage point. His warriors used these very rugged mountains to cover their movements to and from Mexico and to hide when pursued by soldiers. In 1885–86, when General Crook was pursuing Geronimo, he put soldiers here to watch the waterholes. He said his troops guarded every waterhole and trail from the Patagonia Mountains in the west to the Rio Grande in the east.

An information board at Fort Bowie NHS *(Courtesy of the NPS)*

Return to the main road and head north for Willcox on Arizona 186. In about 8 miles turn off the main road and follow the sandy track east to Apache Pass and the car park for Fort Bowie NHS. The path leads along one and a half miles to the ruins of the fort. You literally walk in the footsteps of Cochise and Geronimo. Water is available at the Ranger Station, but make sure you carry some anyway. Apache Pass was a key entrance into southeastern Arizona in the second half of the nineteenth century for settlers, miners, soldiers and many others. It was also a favourite campsite for the Chiricahua. Apache Spring had an-all-year-round water supply.

In 1858 water was a significant factor in the decision by the Butterfield Overland Mail Company to use the pass as part of its route to California. The stage station was a bit like a small fortress, with 12-foot stone walls, a weapons storage room and portholes in the mule corral to shoot from. At first relationships between Cochise and the Americans were peaceful, the celerity wagons stopping to change mules and give passengers a 50-cent meal of bread, coffee, meat and beans. In 1861 the situation changed drastically. Second Lieutenant George Bascom entered Apache Pass to accuse Cochise of stealing cattle from a local rancher and kidnapping the son of a Mexican woman who lived with him. Cochise was affronted, slashed open Bascom's tent and escaped, but the Apaches with him were caught and hanged.

The abandoned Butterfield Overland Mail Company stage station,
Apache Pass, Fort Bowie NHS

The Bascom Affair triggered a long-running war between the Americans and the Apaches which lasted until the final surrender of Geronimo in 1886. The stagecoach service was abandoned. In 1862, when a contingent of soldiers tried to use Apache Pass, it was ambushed by the Apaches who fired from the high ground around the spring. Using howitzers, the soldiers got through to the water supply and forced the Apaches to retreat. A path on this high ground overlooks the whole area and helps you to imagine the battle. The army very quickly built Fort Bowie to keep the pass open. In 1868 the fort was rebuilt more strongly and by the time Geronimo was brought here in 1886, Fort Bowie was a formidable presence in southeastern Arizona.

When Geronimo finally surrendered, he had only 18 warriors with him, including Naiche, the son of Cochise, and 19 women and children. To achieve this surrender thousands of American and Mexican soldiers and 500 Apache scouts had pursued Geronimo over 2,000 miles of desert and mountain terrain. General Crook was replaced by General Miles. Even then it was the news that all of the Chiricahuas were being sent to Florida that shook Geronimo and his men and led them to disarm and go to Fort Bowie. From here they too were sent east. Even the Chiricahua scouts who had helped in the searches for Geronimo were made to go to Florida. These deportations were America's final solution to the Chiricahua menace. These Indians never came back to their homeland.

Willcox to Phoenix (c. 200 miles)

Willcox is a small town on I-10 and a railhead for cattle shipped from the many ranches in the area. Its motels include a Best Western, Days Inn and Super 8, and from here back to Phoenix is an easy day's drive along I-10.

POSTSCRIPT

I made my first long drives in America in 1970-1971. Since then I have been back many times and driven in nearly every part of this huge country. To date I estimate I have driven at least 75,000 miles there. My favourite area is the American Southwest. The bright colours and stark contrasts of its natural landscapes of coastline, forests mountains, deserts and plateaus–themselves all irrevocably marked by the strong presence of prehistoric Indian civilisations, the Spanish and Mormon colonisations of early modern times, and the great westward movement of the American peoples more recently–give the Southwest a unique place in the dramatic and dynamic natural and human history of America as a whole. Stirring landscapes and great historic landmarks make for drives of great interest and enjoyment. I hope that these eight drives in the region inspire you to explore the area. For me they have been some of the best experiences of my life. You don't have to do them all or even choose one drive to do. Pick and mix parts of several drives and have your own adventures. The American Southwest truly is a driver's paradise.

Practical Matters

Rental Cars

1.   In my experience rental companies deal only with automatic and petrol-driven cars.

2.   Use nationwide rental car companies like Alamo, Avis and Budget which have the size, organisation and experience to support you wherever you are. Avoid 'rent-a-wreck' companies.

3.   Choose compact or intermediate cars, according to your budget, the number of people with you and the amount of luggage. Safety, power and comfort are vital during long journeys. Get the best you can afford. Check to make sure that the car has air-conditioning.

4.   Car hire requires your passport, driving licence (have both parts just in case) and a charge card. The minimum age for drivers required by rental companies is usually 25.

5.   Rental agreements provide options for drivers to accept or reject at their discretion. In recent years I have favoured an agreement which covers local taxes, collision damage waiver (CDW), vehicle registration fee, airport/city surcharge, supplementary liability insurance (SLI) and unlimited mileage. Be sure that these things cover you for vehicle fire and theft and third-party insurance.

6.   Check the condition of the car before you leave the rental agency and make sure any marks, dents and scratches on the car's bodywork and interior are recorded by the rental agent and a copy given to you.

Before you drive off

1.   Make sure you know the 24-hour roadside assistance telephone number of your car rental company in case of accident or breakdown.

2.   Make sure you understand all the car's controls and have adjusted the seat and mirrors.

3.   Make sure you know the directions to the main road to start you on your journey.

4.   Remember to drive on the right. Tying a little piece of brightly coloured ribbon on the rim of the steering wheel before you start will remind you each time you get in the car about the need to drive on the right.

Some useful driving tips

1. If stopped by the police remain in the car, wind the driver's window down, put both hands on the wheel and wait until the officer speaks to you. Be polite! Spot fines may be charged.

2. Always keep well topped up with fuel. Road distances can be huge and services limited in the more lonely parts of these drives. Invest in a petrol can and keep that full as well.

3. Pre-payment for fuel is common. Get acquainted quickly with the fuel gauge so that you have an accurate idea of how much petrol you need before filling. It is a nuisance to have to pay again because you are not full up.

4. Do not exceed speed limits. American roads are better policed than British roads. Police cars hide where you cannot see them until it is too late. Radar is widely used – in police cars, helicopters and small planes.

5. In America on two- to four-lane roads it is legal to pass on both sides of a vehicle. Lane discipline is essential. Be most careful when changing lanes and be vigilant about traffic overtaking on the 'inside'.

6. Be very aware of America's school buses – big, single-decker bright yellow vehicles which flash lights when stopped to show that children are getting on or off the vehicle. If lights are flashing, you must stop. This is the case whichever side of the road the bus is on. Children can cross behind or in front of the bus. Do not move until the bus lights stop flashing.

7. Do not park on the sides of highways, within 10 feet of a fire hydrant or in tow-away zones.

8. Do not make U-turns in built-up areas and city centres, or on any road which has a single solid line down the middle.

9. Traffic light sequence is red, green, amber, red. Usually you can filter right on red provided there are no pedestrians there and it is clear of traffic from the left. Traffic lights often hang on wires above the centre of the road rather than standing as fixtures on posts at the roadside as in Britain.

10. Many roads have a left-turn-only central lane for use by traffic going both ways. Keep out of these unless turning left.

11.   Railway (railroad) crossings are indicated by a circular yellow board with black rim, a black cross and the letters RR written on it. Proceed with caution. Look and listen. NB: railway crossings are rarely protected by gates or electronic barriers with flashing lights. Locomotives have to blow their horns when approaching road crossings.

12.   Bright sunshine can be especially dangerous in deserts, so be very careful when you overtake.

American road network

Interstate roads – are exactly what they say they are. Interstate 10 (I-10), for example, stretches from Florida to California. They are motorways (freeways) throughout their length. They have rest areas and service areas. Even-numbered Interstates run east-west, odd-numbered Interstates run north-south. Distances between exits can be long and if you make a mistake you must drive until the next exit. On road signs and maps Interstates are marked with red, white and blue shields.

US Highways – are also federally built roads and extend across state lines. These may be just two- or three-lane roads, or they have motorway sections as well. On road signs and maps US Highways are marked by black lettering on white shields.

State Roads – occur within a state and their numbers change as they cross state boundaries. On road signs and maps State Roads are marked with black letters on white circles.

Business Routes – on Interstates, US Highways and State Roads have 'BUS' in front of the road number.

County Roads – are small, local roads marked with black letters on white squares.

NB: In America drivers follow *route numbers* rather than place names. Route numbers include the direction North, South, East or West, e.g. I-10 West, US 50 East, California 1 North, County 9 South. Know the direction you want to go. If you get it wrong on a freeway, the next turn off could be many miles down the road.

Weather conditions and road reports

Twenty-four-hour television weather programmes provide both national and local information. Make it a daily task to switch on and check this information as it relates to the roads you are driving on.

Each state provides a telephone information service on the current state of its weather and road conditions and these were the numbers in 2010.

ARIZONA:	888-411-7623
CALIFORNIA:	916-445-7623
NEVADA:	877-687-6237
UTAH:	800-492-2400
NEW MEXICO:	800-432-4269
COLORADO:	303-639-1234

Accommodation

Motels are a great American institution. The cheaper ones can look very barrack-like, but all motels offer beds, showers, toilets, telephone and television. In the Southwest open-air pools are common and many motel chains have coin-operated laundries. The more upmarket motels also offer restaurant facilities, but all motels are located near to fast-food restaurants like McDonalds, Kentucky Fried Chicken and Wendy's, and diners like TGI Friday, Applebee and Denny's, which are national chains, or small local concerns like Jerry's Diner or Penny's Diner known to the motel you stay at.

Economy motels include Days Inn, Motel 6, Super 8 and Travelodge. Mid-price motels include Best Western, Comfort Inn, La Quinta Inns, Quality Inn, Ramada Inn and Sleep Inn. These are all national chains and it is easy to book ahead from their reception desks or your room. I have found it very useful to have a selection of motel directories so that I can check if they have a location in the towns I am heading for.

Once on the road you will drive by some national chain motels and it does not take long to pop in and get copies of their directories.

Sometimes there are small towns which do not have nationally known motels. In this book I have given the names and telephone numbers of some of the motels available and the towns' Visitor Centres. In all my years of driving in America I have slept only once in my car.

Few National Parks and National Monuments have accommodation. Where they do, the text includes the appropriate information taken from their 2010 websites.

Final reminder about on-board supplies

As soon as possible when you have left the rental car station, go to a supermarket and buy the following essential supplies which should be replaced if you use any of them during a journey.

- Petrol can and reserve fuel
- Water – a gallon per person
- Food – chocolate, energy bars, dried fruit, fresh fruit, anything not quickly perishable. NB: long-life milk, sugar, plastic cutlery and plastic bowls give the option of boxes of cereals and yoghurts, for example
- First aid box – to include painkillers, sun protection cream, plasters, bandages, safety pins and scissors as well as personal medical supplies
- Protective wear – hat, sunglasses, garments with collars and long sleeves, stout shoes or boots, rain gear, and warm clothes if you are driving in winter.